Circle T
Young C.....

ST.MARY'S UNIVER
A COLLEGE

Circle Time is a simple yet effective strategy proven to be one of the most effective ways of promoting positive behaviour and respectful relationships in Early Years environments.

This highly practical book explains how to put principles for Early Years education into practice through well-structured and purposeful Circle Time-based lesson plans. Jenny Mosley, the UK's leading expert on Circle Time, provides accessible guidance on:

► incorporating the curriculum for personal, social and emotional development
► enabling children to understand universal moral skills
► developing young children's Emotional Intelligence
► helping them to practise problem-solving skills.

Each chapter in this book explains Circle Time in a 'why? what? how?' format, and includes tick-sheets, bullet-pointed pages and plenty of examples of how the rationale works in practice. Early Years practitioners in nurseries, pre-schools and schools will find this an invaluable yet extremely fun approach to teaching young children about their feelings and their relationships.

Jenny Mosley is the founder of the Whole School Quality Circle Time model and Jenny Mosley Consultancies. Her unique approach has featured on BBC Television Teaching Today, Channel 4 and Open University Programmes, in addition to the national press and numerous education journals.

The Nursery World/Routledge Essential Guides for Early Years Practitioners

Books in this series address key issues for early years practitioners working in today's nursery and school environments. Each title is packed full of practical activities, support, advice and guidance, all of which is in line with current government early years policy. The authors use their experience and expertise to write accessibly and informatively, emphasising through the use of case studies the practical aspects of the subject, whilst retaining strong theoretical underpinnings throughout.

These titles will encourage the practitioner and student alike to gain greater confidence and authority in their day-to-day work, offering many illustrative examples of good practice, suggestions for further reading and many invaluable resources. For a handy, clear and inspirational guide to understanding the important and practical issues, the early years practitioner or student need look no further than this series.

Titles in the series:

Circle Time for Young Children
Jenny Mosley

Helping with Behaviour
Sue Roffey

Identifying Additional Learning Needs: listening to the children
Christine Macintyre

Observing, Assessing and Planning for Children in the Early Years
Sandra Smidt

Encouraging Creative Play and Learning (forthcoming)
Diane Rich

Circle Time for Young Children

Jenny Mosley

Routledge
Taylor & Francis Group

LONDON AND NEW YORK

NURSERY
WORLD

First published 2005
by Routledge
2 Park Square, Milton Park, Abingdon, Oxon OX14 4RN

Simultaneously published in the USA and Canada
by Routledge
270 Madison Ave, New York, NY 10016

Routledge is an imprint of the Taylor & Francis Group

© 2005 Jenny Mosley

Typeset in Perpetua and Bell Gothic by
Florence Production Ltd, Stoodleigh, Devon
Printed and bound in Great Britain by
TJ International Ltd, Padstow, Cornwall

British Library Cataloguing in Publication Data
A catalogue record for this book is available from the British Library

Library of Congress Cataloging in Publication Data
A catalog record for this book has been requested

ISBN 0–415–34288–0 (hbk)
ISBN 0–415–34289–9 (pbk)

Contents

Acknowledgements

Thanks to Pat Child, Early Years adviser and author of *Stepping Stones to Success* and *Two Years of Successful Circle Time*, for her invaluable advice and contributions. Also to Ross Grogan for her steadfast support throughout this project.

ILLUSTRATIONS

All illustrations from Meg Mosley except 'Our 5 Skills', p. 41, which is from Mark Cripps.

Introduction

Settling into nursery school is a very important event in many children's lives. For maybe the first time, children and parents must spend their days apart and the child must take their first steps towards independence. They must begin to live as a separate individual and learn how to succeed and be liked in the world away from home. To do this they need to learn how to co-operate and become part of a group of friends and classmates, which can be quite a challenge. This major change is exciting but it can be scary too and each child's experience at nursery needs to be reassuring and responsive. Circle Time is a teaching and learning strategy that offers all Early Years practitioners well-structured and purposeful lesson plans that will enable you to deliver the curriculum for personal, social and emotional development while, at the same time, helping children to understand universal moral values and practise problem-solving skills. Circle Time also facilitates language development, confidence building and the five vital skills of looking, listening, speaking, thinking and concentrating. Children find Circle Time very motivating because it is fast-paced, multi-sensory and very good fun. When engaged in Circle Time activities, they lose their self-consciousness and make developmental strides that can be difficult to achieve in more formal settings.

Using a step-by-step approach, this book is designed to give you a thorough understanding of the ideas that underpin Circle Time before showing you how to lead successful meetings. In Chapter 5 you will find an extensive array of Circle Time session plans that will help you to put these ideas into practice. Soon you will feel confident enough to design your own Circle Time meetings and will find many stimulating ideas in Chapter 6.

Chapter 1

Emotional Intelligence

WHAT ARE SOCIAL, EMOTIONAL AND BEHAVIOURAL SKILLS?

For many years schools have used IQ tests to try and predict which students will do well in both higher education and the workplace. It is now believed that these tests are inadequate and that future success is indicated much more accurately by the measurement of a child's social, emotional and behavioural skills. Research has led experts to believe that success is influenced 20 per cent by IQ and 80 per cent by the various factors that make up a person's character and personality. These are sometimes called 'Emotional Intelligence' or 'social, emotional and behavioural skills' (SEBS) and they form the cornerstone of almost every aspect of our lives.

Social, emotional and behavioural skills are learned, first at home, and then in the wider community of which the school plays an important part. Every child develops at their own pace but high-quality pre-school education can make a considerable difference to children's cognitive, emotional and behavioural development because the foundation for social and emotional success is built in early childhood. If their experience in the nursery is truly nurturing, children can proceed to school feeling competent and ready for the challenges of the 'big school' classroom and beyond. The nursery, with its relaxed, caring and secure environment, offers exciting opportunities for friendship and structured, age-appropriate learning about themselves and others, and children gain all the self-esteem and confidence they need to make sound academic progress and achieve their potential in every aspect of their lives.

1

Social, emotional and behavioural skills are not something that we can teach in a lesson and then forget about. They are personality traits, ways of interacting and a sense of self-worth that grow with us and are nurtured through the ongoing interactions that children have every day with their peers and the adults who surround them. This essential collection of skills and competencies is usually divided into five main strands:

1 Self-awareness
2 Empathy
3 Managing one's emotions
4 Social skills
5 Motivation

These skills are very closely related to one another but every child is different and will acquire them at different rates and with different degrees of success. The earlier they are grasped the better because emotions set the tone of all of our experiences and are what give life its vitality and purpose.

We will now look at each aspect of Emotional Intelligence in a little more depth and see how it relates to your nursery group.

WHAT IS SELF-AWARENESS?

Knowing the **relationship** between **thoughts**, **feelings** and **reactions**.
Knowing **why** we feel that way.
To be able to **communicate** how we are feeling.

Every emotion that we feel is a chain of events that begins with a thought, memory or something that is going on in the world around us. Once the emotion has been activated, a wide range of hormones kick into gear and cause physical changes in our body and we feel our mood change as our heart rate increases and we get hotter or colder or get butterflies in our stomach. These internal changes alter the way we behave and make us cry or laugh or shake with fear.

Somewhere along the way, we become aware that we are experiencing a particular emotion and give it a name so that, when we feel like smiling, we say that we are happy, or when we scowl, clench our fists and feel a strong desire to shout, we label that feeling anger. By the time we are adult, we are able to recognise and name what we are feeling quite precisely. Over time we will have learned a vast array of 'expressive' words that help us finely tune our emotions and we are able to feel very complex mixtures of feelings and give them accurate names. Just think about how you felt as you walked into the interview room when you got your job – there was probably a sense of alert expectation, and a large dollop of hope and confidence, but mixed in there was a sense of nervousness that you might be asked a difficult question. You had a name that covered the whole spectrum of feelings and sensations you were experiencing: you probably called it 'interview nerves' but we all know what you meant.

We are not born with this ability but learn it as we grow. It takes a long time before we reach this mature insight into our own inner lives and the children in your nursery are just beginning their journey towards full emotional self-awareness.

Developing self-awareness in young children

By the time they reach nursery school, most children are likely to be able to identify some of their feelings and tell you about them. In fact, they can be quite assertive about how they feel about the tasks that you wish them to do during each day!

Our task with nursery children is to provide them with an ever-richer vocabulary of 'feeling' words and to help them to accurately relate these words to the sensations and behaviour that each feeling generates. It is a good idea to start with the six 'basic' emotions because these are the ones that we express with our whole face and often our body as well. (The more sophisticated emotions like irritation and doubt are expressed by the eyes alone and take a long time to learn to read.) The six basic emotions are:

- ▶ happiness
- ▶ anger
- ▶ fear
- ▶ calmness
- ▶ interest
- ▶ sadness

3

Our task with nursery children is to provide them with an ever-richer vocabulary of 'feeling' words and help them to accurately relate these words to the sensations and behaviour that each feeling generates. This is done by focusing their attention on the following questions.

- ▶ What am I feeling?
- ▶ How does this emotion feel inside me?
- ▶ What is this feeling called?
- ▶ Why do I feel this way?

Although they need to acquire a rich vocabulary of 'feeling' words, much of your teaching will be interactive and 'on the spot'. Your children will learn best if you can combine 'show' with 'tell' and demonstrate how our face and body language look when we are feeling a particular way. They can then apply what they have seen to their own inner lives in a direct and non-verbal way that circumvents any complications that language generates if it is used on its own.

The following are examples of activities that can be used in the group/classroom either as games or as part of your Circle Time sessions to foster self-awareness in your group.

Box 1.1

MODEL AND MIRROR

Group size	Whole group or small group.
Resources	Pictures of people expressing one of the six basic emotions.
Preparation	You will need to choose one emotion that will be the focus of your lesson.
What to do	1 Choose which emotion you wish to investigate.
	2 Model the body language and facial expression that is appropriate to that emotion.

3   Ask the children to name the emotion that you are modelling.

4   If children give similar words, praise them and repeat the words so that all of the group can learn that there are many ways of expressing the same emotion. It will go like this:

> That's right, Peter, I am acting as if I am very **glad**.
>
> **Glad** is a word that means that I am **happy** that you are feeling so much better and are well enough to come back to nursery/ school.
>
> We're all **joyful**, in fact, because we were worried about you and didn't like to think that you were at home with a nasty pain in your tummy.

Box 1.2

WHAT COULD HAVE HAPPENED TO MAKE ME FEEL THIS WAY?

Group size	Group or whole group.
Resources	None.
Preparation	You will need to choose one emotion that will be the focus of your lesson.
What to do	1 Choose the emotions that you wish to examine.
	2 Use a script like the one here to encourage the children to think about the reasons behind our common emotions.

3   'I am feeling a little bit sad at the moment. How can you tell that I am feeling sad? Yes, that's right, Holly, my mouth is all turned down and my shoulders are hunched up and I have my hands wrapped around my knees. You have noticed all of the things that show how people look when they are sad. Well done!'

4   'What could have happened to make me sad? Can any of you think of something that could have happened to make me look so sad?'

5   'Yes, that's a good suggestion, Paul, and I would be very sad if everyone forgot my birthday and I didn't get a cake.'

6   Obviously, some emotions are easier to discuss than others and you will need to know your group well so that you can protect children who are experiencing difficult events in their home life.

Box 1.3

FEELING TREE

Children will need to be confident and independent with self-registering before this activity is introduced.

Group size	Whole group activity.
Resources	A branch, painted white. A bucket of sand. Plastic eggs (or fluffy balls) in a variety of colours.
Preparation	'Plant' the branch in the sand. Put the eggs in a bowl near the group/classroom door.
What to do	1 First, through discussion with the children, you need to agree on a colour for each 'basic' emotion, perhaps:

▶ Green   full of ideas/interested
▶ Yellow   happy
▶ Blue   sad
▶ Red   angry
▶ Cream   calm
▶ White   afraid

2   Then, as a daily ritual when their name is called, children reply, 'Good morning, Miss, red (or blue, green, etc.).'

3   They then hang their egg on the feeling tree.

4   This little ritual informs you of each child's current mood and, if it is negative, you will be able to give needy children the attention they need to change their egg to a more positive colour.

WHAT IS EMPATHY?

Insight into the **motives, feelings** and **behaviour** of others
and
the **ability to communicate this understanding**.

When we empathise, we are getting inside another person's head and appreciating that they have a different view of the world to our own. This is sometimes called 'perspective-taking' because we try to see things from another person's point of view and identify with their feelings and concerns. We also learn how to 'read between the lines' and see behind the face value of what they are saying and doing. It takes a lot of maturity to do this without our own emotions getting in the way.

Empathy is partly the art of listening unselfishly but most of our emotions are not put into words so we need to able to 'read' a wide range of non-verbal signals such as gestures, facial expression and tone of voice. We all emote constantly and other people's awareness of our mood is usually worked out from these clues. We use these signs to speculate about how someone must be feeling and try to respond appropriately.

We gain many benefits from this constant assessment of the ongoing situation because people who are able to read non-verbal signs tend to be much better adjusted emotionally, and are more popular, outgoing and confident. In other words, they are at ease in social groups.

Not everyone finds it easy to talk about emotions and often we have to use great skill to encourage them to 'open up'. When we do this empathetically we are choosing to put our own concerns to one side and focus on what the other person is saying so that they feel truly heard and understood. Once we have understood how another person feels, we show empathy by acknowledging their state of mind by saying things like, 'I can see you are really uncomfortable about this' or 'Yes, you really have done something to be proud of.' By doing so, we show that we understand another person's mood without actually being in that mood ourselves.

Developing empathy in young children

Our ability to empathise increases the likelihood that we will engage in pro-social behaviour and is now seen as a key characteristic of successful learners. Your goal is not to produce a particular behaviour but to help children see themselves as people who are responsible and caring, and the most effective way to do this is to model empathetic behaviour in all your interactions because children are much more likely to imitate what you are doing than 'do as they are told'. This means that you need to be responsive to them and show that you care about how they are feeling.

The developmental stage of nursery children is characterised by a high level of self-involvement and a tendency to experience and act on empathetic feelings only towards people whom they know well, so it is useful to help them learn how to extend their awareness so that they can come to behave empathetically towards an ever-wider range of people. We do this by showing them just how similar we all are even if we look and dress very differently from one another. This can be modelled in the nursery and children will learn a great deal from the way that you are equally caring and respectful to the different children and adults who come into the group/classroom.

It is a good idea to use activities that start by focusing on each child's own feelings and then show them how to relate these to the feelings of others. This conversation could go a bit like this:

Martin is feeling a little bit excited today because his family is having a barbecue after work and his aunty Sue is going to be there. Meena felt like that a while ago when her cousin came to visit. I feel like that sometimes. I know that something is going to happen and I just can't wait. I keep thinking about it and the waiting seems to take so long that I can hardly stand it.

A chat like this teaches children about empathy because it explains that we all have feelings and other people have similar feelings. It also extends the children's expressive vocabulary and shows them the socially acceptable ways in which we express our feelings, so you need to engage children in this kind of conversation whenever you can.

Role-taking and role-playing activities in which children imagine what it must be like to be another person are very useful. Nursery children are beginning to enjoy imaginative, fantasy play and love to dress up. This gives you many opportunities to focus their attention on how their 'character' must be feeling to behave in the way they do.

The following activities are examples that can be used either as games or as part of your Circle Time sessions to foster empathy in your setting.

Box 1.4

WHAT'S IN THE BOX WITH JEMIMA RABBIT?

Group size	Whole group or small group.
Resources	A cuddly toy. Each time you play this game, you will need a different object that is associated with a particular feeling. (You can use articles that have featured in stories that you have recently read so that the children understand their significance.) These articles could include:

a balloon (because she's excited);
a soggy tissue (because she's upset);
a party hat (because she's happy);
a comfort blanket (because she's feeling shy), etc.

Preparation   Keep Jemima Rabbit in a special box that the children will recognise.

Put a different object into the box each time you play the game.

What to do   This example focuses on the difficult feeling of anger. Use a script like this to guide the children through the game:

> Jemima Rabbit is in the box. Let's take her out and see how she is feeling today.
>
> What's this inside the box with Jemima?
>
> It's a pair of boots!
>
> Why would Jemima want to keep a pair of heavy boots like this?
>
> Let's ask her.
>
> Jemima Rabbit says that these are her special boots. She says that they are kick-a-lot boots.
>
> Oh dear, that sounds a bit scary.
>
> Can any of you think why Jemima Rabbit might feel like wearing kick-a-lot boots?
>
> Yes, she must be feeling very cross. In fact, I think she is angry and that is not a nice feeling.
>
> She says that Toby Bear has made her so angry that she is all steamed up and can't think straight.
>
> Has anyone here ever felt like that?
>
> How did it feel when you were very angry?
>
> Who can guess what Toby Bear might have done to make Jemima so angry?
>
> I don't think that putting on kick-a-lot boots is a good idea. I think that Jemima might get into trouble if she goes round to Toby's house wearing her kick-a-lot boots.
>
> Can anyone tell Jemima a better way of dealing with her feeling of anger?

Let's put those horrible boots into the back of the cupboard and help Jemima to feel calmer.

I know, I'll pass her round the group and you can all give her a nice cuddle and soon she will be feeling calm and happy again.

Pass Jemima round the group and finish the game by confirming that Jemima feels much better now that she has been helped to feel calm.

Box 1.5

MATCHING UP

Group size	Six to eight children.
Resources	Enough large toys for each child to have a go. Enough small things that are appropriate to the emotions and states of mind that you wish to investigate, e.g. a brush, a bandage, a party hat, a blanket, a magic wand.
Preparation	None.
What to do	1 Sit the children in a small circle.
	2 Put the large toys on the floor in the middle of the circle.
	3 Put the small objects on a chair next to you. Show each one to the children and make sure that they understand how they are all used.
	4 Ask a child (Hayley) to choose one large toy and hold it.
	5 Tell the group how the toy is feeling. For example:

George the dinosaur is feeling very sick today. He ate too many green leaves and now his tummy hurts.

11

6   Ask the children to decide which of the range of small objects might help George the dinosaur to feel better. Give this object to Hayley.

7   Praise the children for their kind concern.

8   Repeat this with another big toy by creating another scenario.

9   Continue until each child is holding a large toy and behaving empathetically towards it.

Box 1.6

HOW IS FLUFFY BEAR TODAY?

Group size   Whole group or small group.

Resources   A large fluffy toy.

Preparation   You will need to think of events that will make Fluffy Bear feel a particular emotion. You can use situations that have recently arisen in your setting.

What to do   1   Ask the children to sit on the carpet while you sit with Fluffy Bear on your lap.

2   Use a script like this to describe to the children a situation that you want to focus on.

> Something very wonderful has happened to Fluffy Bear today. He has been asked out to tea with Marybelle. He wants me to brush his fur so that he looks very smart and his Mummy Bear is making a great big plate full of gooey toffee biscuits to give to Marybelle as a present. He likes Marybelle very much. She is his best friend. How do you think Fluffy Bear must be feeling at the moment?

Yes, that's right. Fluffy Bear is feeling very excited and happy. Who can show me how Fluffy Bear is feeling?

Yes, that's right. Fluffy Bear has a great big smile on his face. His mouth is all turned up and his eyes have gone all crinkly.

Can anyone tell me about a time when they felt as happy as Fluffy Bear?

Yes, that's good, Susie, when your dad came home from working away your whole family had big smiles on their faces and I expect their eyes went all crinkly too.

Who can show me a great big smile like that?

Who wants to be very brave and show us how you walk and move about when you are happy. Do you plod around like a big angry giant or do you have another way of walking when you are happy?

Yes, that's right, Wayne, you kind of skip about and feel light and springy and move like you are having a little dance as if you are full of sunshine and fairy cakes.

3   You can make this a daily event and incorporate it into your set routines.

4   When children are expressing emotions, you can refer them back to the work that you did with Fluffy Bear so that they can see how their feelings are 'usual' and are felt by other people, as this develops their social perception skills.

MANAGING EMOTIONS

The ability to **control emotions**
and
express them in a socially acceptable manner.

The ability to manage our emotions to our own benefit is a key skill that ensures that we sustain a sense of emotional well-being despite the difficulties that life throws at us. No one's life ever runs completely smoothly and none of us can predict when something will happen that could overwhelm us in a rush of strong, overpowering emotion. Strong emotions are very destabilising and we can all get caught off guard. Sometimes we need to rein ourselves in and make an effort to rebalance our emotions because we have learned that keeping them in check is socially and personally important.

Most adults have, however, learned to have some control over how long an emotion will dominate their mood and will have found a range of strategies for dealing with bad or uncomfortable feelings. We may get angry but we hold it in until we can let off steam in a controlled manner (or where no one will hear or mind!). We may feel low or miserable but we have ways of soothing ourselves by shopping or playing sport or having a long hot bath surrounded by candles. We know how to make ourselves feel better, calmer or not quite so sad. We resist emotional excess because we know how destructive and exhausting it can be.

This self-mastery puts us in the driver's seat so that we can steer ourselves through life with a degree of control. We don't suppress our feelings or refuse to recognise them but we do manage them to the best of our ability because we have learned that for our emotional lives, at least, the middle road is definitely the most comfortable place to be.

Helping young children to manage their emotions

Children who have a strong sense of emotional well-being will have learned to soothe themselves by dealing with the ups and downs of life in the same way that they have been nurtured and cared for at home. These children are bound to feel less helpless when they come to nursery school. Other children, however, find managing their emotions very difficult and are often overwhelmed by the strength of their feelings.

Their emotions take them by surprise and it can be difficult to guess what they will be feeling next. One minute they are full of the joys of spring, jumping around with enthusiasm, and the next they're convulsed in outbursts of despair or frustration, throwing toys across the floor and collapsing in floods of tears.

When you model how to deal with fierce emotions, you are building their confidence in themselves as self-managing people. The two basic questions that you are helping them with are:

▶   How can I keep my feelings under control?
▶   What is the right way to show this feeling?

The following step-by-step approach will help you to teach self-management skills to the children in your group:

1 Listen and respond with understanding

First, you need to pay close attention to each child and 'mirror' back so that they know they have been understood. For instance, if you suspect that a child feels unable to ask for a go on the playground trike you might ask him what is going on and why he feels nervous by asking quite directly, 'Are you wanting a go on the trike but don't like to go and ask Wayne to share it with you?' If he agrees, you can say, 'It's hard sometimes when you really want a go on something and all the other children seem to get there first.' If you wish, you can use examples from your own life to show him that you understand and that his feeling is not so unusual: 'I feel like that sometimes when I'm out shopping and everyone else seems to get to the nice things first.' Tell him that everyone has these feelings and that they pass. Then offer to help model the right way for him to get what he wants by going over to Wayne and asking if he will share the trike in a few minutes so that everyone can have a go.

2 Help to extend each child's vocabulary of 'feeling' words

It is difficult to manage emotions that we cannot even name and young children often have trouble describing what they feel. You can encourage each child to build a working vocabulary by giving them labels for their feelings. You might say, 'You feel sad because you really want to play on the trike but you never seem to get a chance.' You can also start explaining that sometimes we feel more than one emotion at once and that sometimes these emotions conflict with one another. You might say, 'I know that you were excited about going on the trike but you feel a little bit shy about asking Wayne and now you are disappointed because you're starting to think that you won't ever get a turn.'

3 Confirm what the child is feeling

It doesn't help a child to tell them that there is no reason to be so upset. The feeling is very real to them and they feel it very strongly. You need to acknowledge this and say things like, 'I know that you are feeling very upset that you can't do something that you were looking forward to and I understand how sad you must be feeling.' Talking through emotions works for most children as it does for adults.

4 Be positive

Beliefs have a big impact on the way we act and how we go about doing things. If children believe that they are weak and powerless, they will be constantly giving themselves negative messages and will not 'have a go' even if the situation seems straightforward to you. They need to be given hope and, when you show them how, you are giving them the confidence they need to have a go on their own.

Learning things to soothe oneself when one is sad or upset is an important management skill. So you need to model positive strategies and give praise for the efforts that each child makes in their journey towards understanding and managing their emotions. Saying things like, 'You handled that very well. I was watching how you went up to Wayne and I saw how brave you were being' helps them to internalise positive self-beliefs and is probably the greatest gift you can give to any child.

5 Set a good example

It is important that you check how you are reacting to children because you can be sure that they are watching you. It's important not to be verbally harsh even if your temper is tried to breaking point. Talk about the behaviour but don't label the child or talk about your reaction to it.

'You are a naughty child' or 'You are driving me crazy' are statements that don't help children to learn how to manage their emotions. In fact, they just make them feel more overwhelmed and powerless. It is much better to say things like, 'I can see that you are upset, but hitting Wayne isn't going to help you get a ride on the trike, is it! Do you remember that thing we did in Circle Time? Do you think it might help if you tried that now?'

Another technique is to model how you deal with frustrating experiences. If a child is in a temper, show them how you check out your face, tummy and fists to see if they are tight and then demonstrate how to breathe deeply to blow the anger out. Let the child copy your action and give them praise for taking control. In this way, each child's sense of self-sufficiency is strengthened and they will be more likely to use this strategy in the future.

Some children need to be shown how to minimise their experiences. Saying, 'That wasn't so hard, was it?' helps them to reflect on their growing competency, especially if it is combined with the clear message that perfection is not required – just a brave attempt, which is always worthy of applause.

6 Make your boundaries clear

Self-control and managing our emotions are all about self-discipline. Self-discipline is not something that can be taught in a lesson because it needs to be carefully cultivated over a long period of time. It involves learning to respect oneself and the needs of others and how to act responsibly. This mature sense of self is nurtured through continual, everyday interactions with adults and peers. Without self-discipline children are unable to co-operate, make friends or concentrate on their academic work, so they need to be given a clear set of boundaries, supported by rewards and penalties, when they come into the nursery so that they know what is, and what is not, acceptable behaviour. These involve rules and routines that will be described in Chapter 2 when we look at the Golden Rules.

WHAT ARE SOCIAL SKILLS?

The ability to **influence** other people's emotions in a **positive way**.

17

We are social beings and our ability to mix well in a variety of settings is vital to our emotional well-being. Almost every aspect of our world involves other people and we begin to learn basic social skills very early from the adults at home until we are ready to socialise in the wider world of our school and peer group. Eventually, we are expected to be able to live as autonomous adults who are required to hold their own in the social complexities of modern life.

The six most important social skills that we need to learn during this process are as follows:

1   **Being a good listener** – People love to feel that they have been heard and find good listeners very good company. Good listeners tend to be physically still and attentive and make 'I am listening' noises to show that they are interested and know how to provide feedback to show that they have understood.

2   **Being relaxed and at ease** – When we are anxious, we tend to give out signals that communicate our nervousness to other people. Other people 'catch' our edginess and feel uneasy themselves. Anxiety also works against your being a good listener because it stops you concentrating and really hearing what the other person is saying.

3   **Appropriate eye contact** – If you don't look at someone when you are talking or listening to them they will naturally suppose that you are not truly interested in what they are saying or, worse, that you don't like them. Eye contact varies between cultures but it is important to look interested while not staring.

4   **Interest in and empathy for other people** – When we are self-conscious and preoccupied with our own concerns, we make other people feel that we are not interested in them and they shy away from us. When we concentrate on what someone else has to say, we tend to lose our self-consciousness and make them feel interesting, which benefits everyone and makes the social encounter go more smoothly.

5   **Appropriate self-disclosure** – When we first meet people, it is a good idea to talk about things that are not too personal because small talk puts everyone at their ease. As the relationship progresses, disclosing a little about yourself helps

the other person to feel that you like and trust them and that you are getting to really know one another.

6 **Building rapport** – When a relationship has reached the stage where two people feel that they understand one another and have many shared interests and concerns, we say that they have a rapport. Rapport occurs on an unconscious level and, when it happens, we begin to match one another in the way that we sit and speak and start to look like mirror images of one another. You can speed this process up by consciously copying the way that your friend is sitting or standing, and by reflecting back their language and speech by copying the rate, speed, volume, tone and words. Unconsciously, this will make them feel closer to you and, of course, more friendly!

The social brain can be trained and the earlier we get started the easier our social relationships will be in the future, so it is vital that young children are taught the basics of pro-social behaviour in the nursery schools that they attend.

Developing social skills in young children

By the time that they are 3 years old, many children have quite highly developed social skills. These children will have been raised in nurturing homes where they have learned to trust in their own abilities while being unafraid to ask for help when they need it. In other words, they are confident and have a strong sense of self. Self-confidence is a key feature of socially skilled pre-schoolers because it means that they feel sure that their own needs will be met and are more willing to give emotional space to other children. If you have children in your group who are less confident, you need to be sure that you give them tasks that are just challenging enough to develop their self-assurance without making them give up in frustration. They need praise and more praise so that they can begin to see themselves as capable and successful members of the group.

Another pro-social skill that needs to be learned at this stage of development is self-control. Two aspects of self-control that often need particular attention are the ability to wait and how to share. Many children in this age group easily become overwhelmed by the immediacy of their desires and push forward or lash out at children who get in their way, but you can help them to learn impulse control and empathy when you talk them through their actions using incidents, and model how they can improve their behaviour and still get what they want.

Teaching effective social skills requires you to do two things: first, it is important that all of your work focuses on learning a desirable skill and not on punishing bad behaviour and, second, that you use an approach that shows the child exactly how you wish them to behave through a set of steps that they can manage a bit at a time. Young children learn by watching and practising what adults do, so every time you talk kindly to your children and demonstrate the desired behaviour, you are teaching them to behave kindly towards one another.

The following activities are examples of games you can play with children either in the group or during Circle Time sessions to foster self-management with your children.

Box 1.7

PLEASE AND THANK YOU

Group size	Five to six children.
Resources	A collection of toys.
Preparation	None.
What to do	1 Give every child a toy to hold.
	2 Give them instructions like 'Marianne, **please** put Freddy Frog on your knees.'
	3 When she does so, say, '**Thank you**, Marianne, you have done what I asked you to do, very well.'
	4 When the children have mastered this game you can develop it into a version of 'Simon Says' by telling them to remain perfectly still unless you use the magic word, '**please**'.

Box 1.8

WAITING GAME

This game teaches children to both wait their turn and control their impulse to act immediately.

Group size	Six to eight children.
Resources	A collection of toys.
Preparation	None.
What to do	1 Ask the children to sit in a circle.
	2 Put a range of toys in the middle of the circle.
	3 Explain that each child will be able to choose a toy to play with when you say their name but they must wait until you say the word, '**now**'.
	4 Choose a child like this: 'Janey, please go and choose a toy . . . . now.'

Box 1.9

APPRECIATION GAME

This ritual teaches turn-taking, listening and how to show appreciation.

Group size	Whole group or small group.
Resources	A set of little cards with smiley faces on them (see photocopiable sheet on p. 23).
Preparation	None.
What to do	1 Sit the children in a circle on the floor.

2　Use a script like this to lead the children through the ritual:

> Can you think of anyone who has been kind to you today, Graham?
>
> Can you please tell us about the kind of thing that they did?

(If the child experiences difficulty, you may need to use prompts and say that you noticed how someone was kind.)

> Here is a 'thank you' card. Would you like to give it to Honeylou and say 'thank you' to her for helping you with the tidying up?

3　Reinforce Graham's message by giving Honeylou a big 'thank you' from the rest of the group and maybe a clap too.

WHAT IS MOTIVATION?

The **belief** that you can successfully reach your **goals**
and
the **willingness to persist** and overcome setbacks.

The word motivate comes from the root word 'to move' and is all about how we choose not to be lazy and decide to get something done. If you have been on a long walk on a hot day, you will be very motivated to go and get a drink, for instance. Motivation gives us a special kind of energy that pushes us into a place where we want to be. It makes us purposeful and goal-directed. When we are motivated, we 'go for it' and won't let anything stop us, but, when we are demotivated, we give up easily and find all kinds of reasons to avoid the effort that achieving our goals will involve. Motivation gives us the strength to do unpleasant or painful things just as dancers and musicians must practise the same moves over and over again until they are perfect. It's what gives students the patience to study and revise until they are certain that they are ready

to pass an exam because we can only overcome setbacks and frustrations if our motivation towards a goal outweighs the forces that are working against it.

Healthy motivation is an emotional skill because it is profoundly affected by how we feel about ourselves. The key to healthy motivation is the knowledge that we can achieve because we are more than capable of getting to where we want to be if we decide to make the effort. The degree to which we are motivated is a measure of our self-esteem because it requires that we believe in ourselves and that we are full of enough hope and optimism to see us through the hard times.

Developing motivation in young children

When we are very young, our self-esteem and belief that we are capable and full of potential is an indication of the feedback and nurturing that we have received from the adults around us. The children who come to your nursery will all be different but they will each already have some strong ideas about what their capabilities are. You, too, will quickly make judgements about them based on your observations and interactions with them. It is important to remember that ability is not a fixed thing. Children's (and adults') beliefs about their abilities have a profound effect on those abilities, so it is important to work on the self-esteem of children who seem demotivated so that you can begin to change their self-image and help them to see themselves in a more positive light.

People who feel good about themselves are the ones who bounce back from failures and approach things in terms of how to handle them rather than worrying about what might go wrong, so if you see a child who is clearly nervous, you need to be sure that you are there to encourage and reassure them without taking over. Young children tend to interpret too much assistance as an indication that they lack ability, so offer guidance, praise effort and persistence, but let them try hard on their own.

Healthy motivation is based on each child's belief that they have the ability to achieve and that the effort will be worth the reward. The following activities will give them experience of this concept and also give them real understanding of the appropriate words that they will need in the future. They can be used either as games or as part of your Circle Time sessions to foster motivation in your group.

Box 1.10

WORTH THE EFFORT

Group size	The whole group can participate or you can do this activity with a small group – it works both ways.
Resources	A collection of small toys. A 'treat' like a song or special game they love.
Preparation	Put the toys where they can be seen at the far end of the room. Space them out so that they are not too easy to find.
What to do	1 Ask the children to sit on the carpet and tell them that you are going to give them a special group treat if they manage to play a hard game.
	2 Send one child at a time to fetch one of the toys.
	3 'Sam, I want you to go and fetch Mr Teddy.'
	4 Add instructions to make the journey more interesting, e.g. 'I want you to fetch Mr Teddy but you must crawl under the tables on the way there.'
	5 Send other children to fetch different toys and make it just a little bit difficult for each one.
	6 When all the toys have been retrieved you can say, 'That wasn't easy because you had to crawl under the tables but all that hard work was worth it because now we can have our treat.'
	7 Another way of playing this game is to put pieces of fruit in bowls and ask the children to go and fetch them. When you have all the bowls, you can share the fruit and make the same point.

25

Box 1.11

STORY TIME

Group size Whole group.

Resources Stories from your group collection.

Preparation None.

What to do You will need to be familiar with the story you are going to read. Traditional stories work well for this activity – all you have to do is remember to make the points that you wish to make when you are talking about the story with your children.

Research has shown that stories have an impact on the behaviour of nursery school children, so use them to illustrate what characters achieve through motivation. For example, the little pig who made the most effort and built his house from bricks was the one who finished up with the home that kept out the wolf. He built the house **all by himself** and worked hard to make sure that it was safe. All his hard work certainly paid off.

Top tip – Avoid gender bias and make sure that you read stories where girls are active, effective and achieving.

How are you, Fluffy Bear?

Being motivated to succeed often means that we must sustain our effort over a long period of time. It helps if we celebrate every little step forward. Use a group/classroom toy to show the children how this works. Here is a script that uses this idea:

Hello, Fluffy Bear. How are you today?

Oh dear, Fluffy Bear is a bit worried. He's just found out that there are 26 letters in the alphabet and that he will need to learn every one before he can be a good reader. Don't worry, Fluffy Bear. You don't have to learn them all at once. You just have to learn them one at a time and, if you keep going and don't give up, one day you will wake up and realise that you know all of them.

Next day – Hello Fluffy Bear. How are you today? Fluffy Bear says that he learned all about 'A' today. He says 'A' looks like this, etc.

Well done, Fluffy Bear. That's clever of you and you have tried hard today.

If you chart Fluffy Bear's progress every day, the children will soon see how persistent effort accrues to make real achievement.

Top tip – Events like this can be turned into daily rituals. Familiar rituals are very reassuring for children.

All by myself

Motivated people feel that they are in control of their lives. They believe in their ability to get things done. Sit the children in a circle and ask questions like:

Who can brush their own teeth?

Would you like to show us how you do it, Keith?

Well done, we can all see that you brush your teeth all by yourself. I bet you couldn't do that when you were at playschool but now you can. You are getting more and more independent, aren't you?

Use smiley-face stickers so that everyone can celebrate as a child gains autonomy. You can also make 'letters' for children to take home so that parents can celebrate their children's stride towards autonomy. For example:

All By Myself

I put on my socks today.

WHAT IS SELF-ESTEEM?

Self-esteem is an experience that involves our whole being. When our self-esteem is healthy, we feel pleased to be who we are and this sense of liking ourselves makes us energetic, confident and sociable. When we look in the mirror, we see someone who deserves to be happy, liked and loved and we feel that we have all the positive strength to get what we need from life. We expect to be liked so we are relaxed, open and friendly with people whom we meet and, what is more, we find that they are relaxed in our company because we have no hidden agendas.

Adults who have been raised to have consistently high self-esteem are extremely lucky because their strong core makes it possible to bounce back from setbacks as they firmly believe that they are worthy of the good things that life has to offer. People who feel good about themselves are motivated to increase their self-esteem and seek personal growth, development and improvement by exercising their capabilities. Such people benefit from social interaction and enjoy making new contacts.

People with low self-esteem, on the other hand, are forced to constantly fight against the fear that they are unworthy of love and success and that they are stupid and helpless and that the world may well be against them. Sometimes, they believe this so strongly that they reject praise and encouragement because it unsettles their picture of themselves as people who can never receive such treasures. They tend to feel awkward, shy, conspicuous and unable to express themselves. They worry about making mistakes, being embarrassed or exposing themselves to ridicule. Often they compound their problems by opting for avoidance strategies because they are convinced that whatever they do will result in failure and further demoralisation. Conversely, they may overcompensate for their lack of self-esteem by becoming boastful and arrogant to cover up for their sense of unworthiness. Their tendency to look for evidence of inadequacy immobilises them and they are resistant to change because they see it as threatening and risky. They are people who feel that they have no control over their lives and this makes them account for their successes by finding reasons that are outside themselves – 'I got lucky', 'someone helped me'. As a result, they are unable to ever appreciate the true extent of their capabilities.

Self-esteem is clearly implicated in the achievement process and variations in self-esteem are closely related to the ability of many children to benefit from their education, and the nursery can have a significant effect upon the self-esteem of many of the more vulnerable children in our society.

Building self-esteem in the nursery

Our level of self-esteem is not something that is fixed at birth and is profoundly affected by the experience of acceptance and encouragement that we receive from other people. By the time they reach your nursery, each child you encounter will have begun to form quite a clear picture of themselves and the differences between their levels of self-esteem will be obvious to you almost as they walk through the door. Children whose self-esteem has been nourished will be self-assured and easy to like, which will tend to make you warm to them and, in turn, will nurture their healthy level of self-esteem. Those with a shattered sense of self-worth may be more complicated and difficult. Without proactive intervention, these are the children who are in danger of growing up to be envious, self-destructive, unhappy adults. These children offer you a breathtaking opportunity because, if you are able to strengthen their belief in themselves, you will have played a vital part in changing the direction of their whole lives.

The essence of your role in the nursery school is to provide an environment where children have the opportunity to experience personal success and feel secure in the knowledge that you will be consistently looking for ways to make them feel good about themselves. The following 14 'rules' sum up how this can be done and how you can help children to possess the high levels of self-esteem that will make them strong, happy and successful.

Speak in language they understand – not too grown-up, not too babyish.
Tell them they are capable, strong and wonderful.
Respond with warmth, patience and interest.
Openly appreciate their efforts and achievements.
Nourish their potential to be unique and let them 'be themselves'.
Give them positive feedback, 'I like you because ____.'

29

Celebrate every small step towards independence.

Help them learn to see setbacks and mistakes as learning experiences.

Include them in the adult world by letting them help with chores and decision-making.

Listen with respect and interest.

Discipline by reward for good behaviour and punish only very rarely.

Respect their right to have their own opinions.

Encourage them to feel independent.

Nurture their sense of mastery by giving them attainable goals.

The following activities can be used as part of your Circle Time sessions and adapted to suit the needs of your particular group.

Box 1.12

ROUND AND ROUND

Group size	Six to ten children.
Resources	A chair for each child plus one extra chair.
Preparation	None.
What to do	1 Put the chairs in a circle.
	2 Ask the children to choose a chair and sit down.
	3 Ask the child sitting to the right of the extra chair to say: 'I would like ___ to come and sit next to me because ___ .'
	4 The child then says something nice about the child they choose.
	5 The named child then moves to the empty chair.
	6 The child sitting to the right of the new empty chair then continues the game.

7 Be vigilant and give prompts when necessary. Ensure that every child is chosen. You can always join in to make certain that this happens.

Box 1.13

ZOO GAME

Group size   Group or whole class.

Resources   A beanbag or 'passing' object.

Preparation   None.

What to do   1   Lead the children in a few animal actions so that they understand what is required of them. These could include: pretending to fly, hopping like a frog, beating the chest like a gorilla.

2   Ask the children to join in this rhyme while passing the object round the group:

Monkey, lion, kangaroo
All the animals in the zoo
Have a look. See what I can do.

3   The child who is holding the passing object when the rhyme ends stands up and shows the children an animal action.

4   The other children clap, guess the animal's name and then join in the action.

5   Repeat 1–4 until everyone has had a go.

6   Very shy children may need a partner (you!) but should receive a clap, etc. for having a go.

Box 1.14

HI NOTES

Group size	Group or whole class.
Resources	Some happy music.
Preparation	Have a CD player ready.
What to do	1 Play the music and encourage the children to dance and jig about.
	2 Stop the music and ask the children to smile at someone near to them and say, 'Hello, how are you today?' To which the other child replies, 'I'm fine thanks.'
	3 Continue until you feel that the children are tiring.
	4 If any children are shy you can give them cuddly toys or puppets that will 'speak' on their behalf.

Box 1.15

THIS BELONGS TO ONE OF US

Group size	Four to eight children.
Resources	An item from a few of your children (coat, school bag, shoe, sock, etc.). A sack or big bag.
Preparation	None.
What to do	1 Hide the items in the bag or sack.
	2 Ask the children to sit in a circle.

3   Put your hands in the sack and tell the children that you are holding an item that belongs to one of the children. Keep the item hidden in the sack.

4   Tell the children that they have to guess who it belongs to and that you will give them some clues.

5   Say really positive things about the child – lovely brown eyes, a beautiful smile, etc.

6   When you have said enough positive things, give the children a look at the item and ask them to guess who you have been talking about.

7   Repeat your compliments as you return the item to the child.

8   Do this with a few children each day until everyone has had a turn.

Chapter 2

Moral values – the Golden Rules

WHAT ARE MORAL VALUES?

Humans are sociable beings and like to live together in groups or communities. If these communities are to work well, we need look after one another and ensure that each member of the group is treated with consideration. These agreements about the 'rules' that should underpin and guide our behaviour towards each other are called our moral values. Whether an action is described as moral or immoral, right or wrong, is dependent on the effect it has on the welfare of other people. We learn moral values from the people who surround us and eventually we internalise them and many of our emotions are associated with how well we feel we have kept, or failed to keep, the codes of moral behaviour that we learned when we were young.

Teaching moral values to young children

Circle Time uses six Golden Rules to teach moral values. These rules set straightforward standards of behaviour that must be kept in every situation. It is important that they are maintained at all times by all members of the school community because it is not sufficient to teach the rules and to display them on the group/classroom walls if they are not the rules that are modelled in real life. The Golden Rules bring concepts of morality and responsibility into the forefront of children's minds and enable them to become more aware of their right to speak, and their responsibility to listen.

The Golden Rules used in infant and primary schools are:

We are gentle, we do not hurt anybody.
We are kind and helpful, we do not hurt people's feelings.
We are honest, we do not cover up the truth.
We try to work hard, we do not waste time.
We look after property, we do not waste or damage things.
We listen to people, we do not interrupt.

These are too complicated for young children, so in the nursery it is better to start with one or two positive statements:

We are gentle.
We are kind and helpful.

Generally speaking, the other Golden Rules are gradually introduced from the second term of reception onwards. You will find example meeting plans for all of the Golden Rules later on in the book (see pp. 87–98). A further Golden Rule that is useful for young children is:

We play well, we do not spoil each others' games.

For nursery children, it is useful to make a display from photographs of children modelling the required good behaviour and then attention can be drawn to the desired behaviour with a visual example.

Teaching moral behaviour is a **what, why, how** process:

What e.g. The rule is, we are kind and helpful.
Why e.g. How do we feel when someone is kind to us?
How do we feel when someone hurts us?
How We teach how by:

▶ **Modelling** expected behaviours – practising what we preach and preaching what we practise. The behaviour that you are willing to tolerate in your 'lived in' group/classroom is the real set of rules that your children will keep. It is no good to tell children that they must talk politely to one another if you shout at them, for instance. If your words match your actions, you are teaching children to take words seriously and to internalise the rules behind them. If your

35

words are not matched by your behaviour, it is likely that the children will ignore the words and build their morality on their experience of your personal actions.

▶ Setting up **incentive and sanction systems** that reinforce the lessons that we wish children to learn. Moral rules are best reinforced through praise and reward. Some adults pay so much attention to poor behaviour that they inadvertently give the message to children that the best way to get attention is to behave badly. It is also important that children see the rewards for good behaviour as worthwhile. Real rewards that can be held and taken home suit young children very well and have the advantage of being transportable to the larger environment outside the nursery where they can be shared with family and friends and stuck on the fridge to everybody's delight. These include badges, stickers, stamps, letters and certificates. These mount up in the child's kitchen or bedroom and give them constant positive feedback and pride.

▶ **Golden Time / Privilege Time** is an effective system of rewards, or celebration, and sanctions that works successfully with nursery-age children. Participation in the system teaches children that communities are prepared to put time and effort into safeguarding their moral values. With clear rules backed by simple incentive / sanction procedures, children learn that rewards are something that we earn and that unacceptable behaviour has consequences that are predictable, consistent
and fair.

Setting up and carrying out Golden Time

1 Set the scene by introducing and reinforcing the Golden Rules and any group / classroom or safety rules, simplified as much as necessary at first. Make sure the children all understand them and display them using photographs and pictures to illustrate.

2 Make your intentions very clear, telling the children that you believe that they are all capable of keeping the Golden Rules and that you want to reward them every day for keeping the rules so well. You may prefer to call Golden Time a 'celebration'.

3   When establishing the practical side of Golden Time, ensure
    that it has its own timetabled slot. Ten minutes per day, with
    a slightly longer session towards the end of the week for
    more involved activities, is recommended for Early Years
    children.

4   For Golden Time to be effective, it is essential that the activities
    on offer really are special and are not available at any other
    time. These can be whole-group activities like dancing or party
    games or they can be games, construction kits or clay modelling
    that are kept especially for Golden Time. A special box of toys
    or games can be put aside.

5   You will need to vary the activities from time to time so that
    children are always excited by the prospect of their special
    reward for good behaviour. As the children's tastes develop, you
    will need to adapt your activities accordingly. Circle Time is an
    excellent opportunity to work out what is currently motivating
    the children.

If a child breaks a Golden Rule:

1   Children who have broken the rules lose their right to
    participate in some or all of this precious time.

2   You need to make a large, yellow sun with a smiley face on it.
    The rays of the sun are yellow clothes pegs, but the reverse side
    of each peg is painted grey. Each child's name is printed on the
    yellow side of the peg, along with a small photograph of the
    child's face. The sun represents Golden Time and shows the
    faces of all the children who have kept the Golden Rules and
    are going to enjoy the privilege.

3   If a child breaks a Golden Rule, they are initially given a
    'knowing look', followed by a verbal warning. If they fail to
    respond, their peg is removed from the yellow sun and placed
    on a large picture that is half sun and half cloud. This stage
    offers the child a choice: to heed the warning and be reinstated
    on the yellow sun or to be removed to a large picture of a sad,
    grey cloud and lose Golden Time. It is important to be sure that
    the child realises it is a choice that they now need to make. If
    they do not understand, your system will not work and it will
    confuse and frustrate the child.

37

If the child continues to break a Golden Rule, their peg is placed on the sad, grey cloud and the child loses one minute of Golden Time. A private note is made of this by the practitioner. If they then keep the rules until the next break time, or until the end of the session for very young children, their peg is replaced back on the smiley sun but there is still a note made that they have lost one minute of Golden Time.

4   If they break the Golden Rule again, they are again faced with the sun/cloud choice and the child faces losing another minute and so on. The child needs to be aware of when the time to choose behaviours is, so that they can correct this behaviour.

5   When Golden Time begins, any child who has lost Golden Time will sit at a table near the activity area. A sand-timer on the table is used to show the child how long they must remain seated before being allowed to join in the fun. Sitting and watching the timer quietly is more effective if other children are enjoying themselves nearby.

6   If the child ruins the quiet minute of sitting, the sand-timer is turned over to start again, with the reason given to the individual child.

7   It is important that, once the child has finished the one minute, they are welcomed back into the circle with a big smile and a 'Well done'. Children love party games as a Golden Time choice: musical statues, sleeping lions, etc. When the child is welcomed back, they will still have nine minutes left of lovely fun!

Golden Time works best with Early Years children when:

▶   The children all understand the Golden Rules (even if there are only two to start with), and they are displayed clearly.

▶   The children look forward to Golden Time and it is spoken about and prepared for in an exciting and meaningful way.

▶   The activities on offer are valued by the children and they can choose to vary their activities.

▶   The celebration is enhanced by a celebration banner, special golden material, special glittery crafts or anything sparkly, out of the ordinary or lavish-looking.

► Activities are varied between independent, paired and group sessions.

► The display of the sun and cloud system is very bright and clear, and understood by all the children.

► The system of using the pegs, choosing the behaviour and losing Golden Time is very consistently adhered to. Consistency is one of the keys to its success.

► All the adults use the same system.

► All the pegs start off on the sun symbol, and are replaced on the sun symbol when the next break, lunch or end of the day arrives, so that parents always see their child's name on the sun and every child starts each new session with a clean slate.

Chapter 3

Learning skills

WHAT ARE LEARNING SKILLS?

We can't see what is going on inside someone else's brain but we know someone has learned something when we are able to observe a fairly permanent change in his or her performance. In other words, if they are able to do something today that they couldn't do yesterday, we will decide that they have grasped what they need to know and have stored it in their memory and have it available for future use. Whether we are able to learn something quickly or with difficulty is, to some extent, dependent on how skilful we are at getting organised and studying effectively. Children in the nursery are usually very eager to explore and learn and all you need to do is harness their curiosity and enthusiasm and help to learn the attitudes and organisational skills that will ensure they achieve their potential as learners.

In nursery groups these skills are practised at the beginning of each Circle Time session in the following way:

▶ **Looking** – 'In Circle Time we use our looking skills.' Point to eyes.
▶ **Listening** – 'We use our listening skills.' Point to ears.
▶ **Speaking** – 'We use our speaking skills.' Point to mouth.
▶ **Thinking** – 'We use our thinking skills.' Place hands on side of head.

When the children are secure with these four skills, introduce the fifth skill:

Looking

Our
5
Skills

Listening

Concentrating

Speaking

Thinking

▶ **Concentrating** – 'We use our concentrating skills.' Clasp hands and place on laps and look at teacher.

These skills can be learned by young children if you make a conscious point of modelling and describing them as you work through each activity during the day and in Circle Time sessions. The following tips will help you teach them effectively:

▶ **Show them how you break down tasks into parts.** For instance, you can talk through getting out a puzzle by giving a running commentary like this: 'First we will go and find the box. Now we need to open the box and carefully take out all the pieces. Let's put all the pieces on the table and have a look at each one. Now we can start to put them together. This looks like the front end of the tractor. Can you see the back end?', etc. (Looking, Listening, Thinking)

▶ **Show how we collect everything we need before we start a task.** 'Let's do some drawing. What will we need to find before we can start? Yes, we will need to get some paper and crayons. Let's put them on the table. Do you think that we have the right colours or are there some missing? Yes, we need to find a pink one if we are going to do a picture of a fairy. Do you know where we might find a pink crayon? I saw Mary using one a little while ago, maybe she has finished with it now and we can go and get it from her table.' (Looking, Speaking)

▶ **Finish each task before going on to another.** Some children like to flit from one activity to another and are in danger of becoming poor learners as a result. With young children it may be necessary to allow them to cut an activity short but they need to experience a proper sense of closure if they are to come to understand that we all need to learn to finish what we start. (Thinking, Concentrating)

▶ **Extend periods of concentration.** Concentration is a vital learning skill and children need to be shown that this can be extended through practice. Use a sand-timer for children who find this difficult and tell them that they must stay on task until the timer says that they can stop. Make sure that you remove unnecessary distractions and tell the children what you are doing by saying things like: 'I can see that you need some peace and quiet while you look at the books. Why don't we ask Susie to take her toys outside and we'll switch off the music because we can't concentrate when it is playing can we?' (Concentrating)

▶ **Disorganised children are often indecisive.** Some children find it very hard to make up their minds about which activity they want to do and they need to be coached to make decisions and stick to them. 'Now, Joshua, if you can't decide whether to build with the blocks or to paint a picture, why don't we make a plan. You could play with the blocks until snack time and then you could do your painting. If you get started straight away, you will have plenty of time to do both.' (Thinking, Concentrating)

▶ **Help children to organise their thoughts** by encouraging them to talk about their day-to-day experiences. This helps them to think in a sequential way. You can help them by clarifying and summarising as you go along and use prompts if they get in a muddle but it is more instructive to ask questions than to provide them with answers. (Thinking, Speaking)

▶ **Use posters and pictures to show children how to focus their attention when they are looking.** When you point out details and show how pictures can tell a story, you are teaching children how to look in a discerning and informative way. With individual children, you can do this with smaller pictures in story books. (Looking, Thinking)

▶ **Model the body language of attentive listening.** When we are attentive, we listen with our whole body and mind. You can model this behaviour when you listen to children speak in circle meetings. When people listen to us in this way we feel that we have truly been heard and this is very affirmative and has a major impact on our sense of well-being. (Listening)

▶ **Modulate your voice when you speak.** If you wish to hold children's attention, you need to ensure that you use your voice like a musical instrument. Change the tempo, speak quietly or more loudly and use your whole body to convey your message. This ensures that you will hold their attention and they will be much more likely to absorb the lesson that you are teaching. (Speaking)

Chapter 4

How to deliver Quality Circle Time meetings

WHAT IS CIRCLE TIME?

Circle Time is a group approach to learning moral values and social, emotional and behavioural skills. Children and adults work together to solve problems and raise one another's self-esteem and each individual contributes to the group and feels supported by other members. This helps everyone to work as a team that celebrates difference in others and respects their values and beliefs.

The aim of Circle Time is to nurture the social and emotional growth of each child while increasing their empathetic understanding of other people's viewpoints. It is a democratic listening system designed to enhance children's sense of safety by offering them the opportunity to discuss their concerns and to practise pro-social behaviour in an enjoyable and stimulating way. In doing so, it encourages the development of effective communication and reduces anxiety and social isolation. The effect of regular circle meetings is that the children are emotionally strengthened and are, therefore, better able to cope with the stresses and strains of life.

The prescribed curriculum for personal, social and emotional development can easily be adapted to the Circle Time approach and other elements of the curriculum are often incorporated into meetings with great success.

Circle Time activities should always be presented in a planned, structured way, but teachers are encouraged to be flexible and find their own creative approach to their delivery. Each circle meeting has five steps that take the group through an introductory phase that relaxes them and prepares them for the middle phase, which is an open forum when the key issues of the session are introduced. During this phase, children also participate in discussions or activities that are designed to increase their understanding and strengthen their self-esteem. The meeting then draws to a close where they engage in activities that lighten the mood and ensure that everyone feels safe and comfortable.

The five stages are:

▶ **Meeting up** – This can be a fun warm-up to help children relax, release tension and feel the joy of being together with each other. These starting rituals are vital to create the right supportive atmosphere and are often used to encourage the children to sit next to other children who are not their usual companions. For some groups/classes it is best not to start with a highly energetic game and a more calming game like passing around a tambourine without it making a noise is more appropriate. This choice is left to the expertise of the practitioner who knows their group well.

▶ **Warming up** – In order to encourage children to listen to each other, a verbal activity is introduced. This is called a 'round' and the teacher begins a sentence that must be repeated and completed by each child. The teacher should say their part without any show of emotion so that the child can give their own thoughts. An example of this would be the completion of a sentence like, 'The animal I would like to be is ____.' A 'talking object' is used to show whose turn it is to speak and whoever is holding the talking object has the right to speak uninterrupted. The talking object is then passed to the next person. The talking object needs be small enough for little hands to hold and some nurseries use an egg or a small fluffy toy (Talking Teddy). Alternatively, you may decide to use a different object each week by choosing something that is related to your current theme or the letter of the alphabet that you are encouraging your children to learn. Holding the talking object does not oblige anyone to speak and any child who does not wish to do so may say 'pass' and hand it on.

▶ **Opening up** – This is the key stage of the circle meeting and represents an opportunity for discussion or for activities designed to develop children's understanding of key social, emotional or behavioural issues. Drama and role-play activities are often used in the nursery during this phase and any subject that seems relevant to the needs of the group can be introduced and explored. This middle phase is vital for encouraging children to develop a belief in their ability to make responsible choices and decisions.

► **Cheering up** – It is important to help children move away from the issues of concern raised in the middle phase and the cheering up stage is used to celebrate the group's successes and strengths and to give praise and thanks to one another.

► **Calming down** – Each meeting should end with a closing ritual and this winding down phase is quiet and calm and ensures that a proper feeling of closure is achieved.

Initially, staffs are advised to use the fail-safe sessions that have been devised by experienced Circle Time practitioners. By working through these lesson plans, you will gain confidence and become able to extend your creativity, spontaneity and imagination and devise meetings that are tailored to the particular needs of your group. Puppets, cloaks, a treasure chest, blindfolds and other props can then be used to ensure that meetings are never dull and that children come to each meeting with a sense of joyful anticipation and to help you to be sure that their attention will be held throughout the meeting.

GETTING READY FOR CIRCLE TIME

You will need a carpeted area for your circle meetings. This needs to be large enough for the children to sit in the circle and engage in the activities that happen inside it. Some children will take a while to get used to sitting in the circle and giving their full attention to what is going on but it helps if you can show them where they sit by providing carpet squares, cushions or small chairs. You will need to clear this space of anything that might distract them and may find it useful to have a symbolic ritual that shows the children that Circle Time is about to begin. For instance, some teachers put a paper doily in the middle of the circle before the meeting begins.

Circle Time should be timetabled at least once a week but nursery children may need shorter meetings more frequently. You may wish to introduce the children to the idea of Circle Time by holding meetings

that last for about 10 minutes and increase this time to 15–20 minutes as they become more accustomed to what happens. Also, start with the children sitting on the floor and build up to using the chairs. The time for this is best decided by the practitioner, as and when the children are ready.

It is important that you choose a time when you are all feeling positive and upbeat because your meetings will not go well if you are stressed and the children are tired. Children's emotional and social development is so important that it justifies a prominent place in the curriculum and meetings should not be slotted in at a time when everyone is not at their best.

Circle size

To begin with, you need to keep the group numbers small. Six children make a good group size for the initial meetings. This can be increased to 10–12 once everyone is familiar with the rules and routines. Eventually you can work towards holding full group meetings but these are more difficult to manage in the nursery and their success will depend on the children's prior experience and your expertise in holding meetings.

Adult helpers

You should not try to hold circle meetings with nursery children unaided and will probably need at least one adult helper to assist you. It is useful if each adult helper is familiar with the plan that you intend to use and is designated a specific role, such as sitting with a child who may find the concentration required difficult to sustain. Alternatively, they may wish to sit with shy or anxious children who need encouragement and prompts if they are to contribute their ideas with confidence. Parents can gain a lot from attending circle meetings and you may decide to distribute invitations so that they feel welcome to come and join in.

It is fundamental to the philosophy of Circle Time that all children are valued for the unique people that they are and it is important that those with special needs are accommodated and given the extra support that will enable them to participate as fully as possible. This may well mean one-to-one support from an adult helper. For children whose development is delayed it is important that you have strategies ready to simplify the activities so that these children understand what is expected of them.

Make the ground rules clear

Children need to be made very aware of the ground rules if meetings are to run smoothly. They will get used to them very quickly but in the beginning you will need to run through them before every meeting. Thereafter they will probably only need the occasional reminder. These are the ground rules:

> ► **We will not interrupt. We will listen carefully to everybody else.** We will use the 'talking object' or put up our hands when we wish to speak. Attentive listening is a vital social skill and meetings cannot be successful if this rule is not observed. Sometimes, you will need to interrupt but you need

to do this very politely: 'I very sorry to have to interrupt you, Sally, but I just need to remind Akbar that he needs to look at you when you are speaking.'

▶ **No put-downs.** Children will clam up and refuse to contribute if they feel that their views will be dismissed or laughed at. Circle meetings are all about reinforcing good behaviour and it is important that only positive things are said. Children should not ridicule or laugh at one another and need to learn how to be kind to each other.

▶ **Everyone has the right to 'pass'.** In the circle, every child has an equal right to speak but also has the right to remain quiet if they so wish. Children can say 'pass' if it is a round. You can give them another opportunity to speak at the end of each phase when you can say, 'Does anyone want to change their mind and say something before we move on?'

Top tip – Quiet or shy children can often be persuaded to participate if you give them a puppet to hold. You can then ask the puppet to join in the session and ask the child to speak on the puppet's behalf!

Maintaining the positive atmosphere

You need to be proactive and model the behaviours that you wish to instil in your children, so make sure that you have a range of positive rewards ready before each meeting. Be ready to give praise and more praise and make sure that you have a list of specific acts and behaviours that you can celebrate during the meeting. No opportunity to give positive feedback should be missed and it is very easy during a busy week to forget that you noticed some small achievement, so it is a good idea to keep a notebook in your pocket so that you can jot down things that you observe. It is also important that you do not neglect children who are always good and many teachers find that keeping a little register of praise given ensures that it is distributed fairly.

If a child is continually disruptive a visual warning can be used. You can make a number of cards that have a sad face drawn on one side and a happy face on the other. Keep these cards handy so that you can place one beside a child who is spoiling the meeting. Tell them that the face is sad because they have made the whole group sad by breaking an important rule. If the child responds positively and begins to behave well, you can smile and turn the card over and explain that everyone is now pleased with them. If the child is unable to change their behaviour, they are asked to sit outside the circle and watch a one-minute sand-timer before being asked if they are ready to rejoin the group.

It is important for the effectiveness of Circle Time that you remain enthusiastic and vibrant, so it is vital that you review the quality of your meetings regularly to ensure that they have not lost their lustre and become tired and boring. To avoid this you need to plan well and ensure that your meetings are closely matched to your learning objectives. Start every meeting with a reminder about the five skills of looking, listening, speaking, thinking and concentrating because this will ensure that you (as well as the children) are clear about the attitudes that underpin the social, emotional and behavioural skills that you are wishing to investigate during each meeting.

Chapter 5

Circle Time sessions

HOW TO USE THE SESSION PLANS

Most of the circle meeting plans that follow contain the full five stages as described previously. Some nursery children may find this too tiring and you may decide to cut out some of the stages. It is vital that each meeting has a clear beginning, a focused middle and a positive, upbeat closure but, so long as you keep to that basic structure, you can modify each plan to meet the needs of your particular group of children. There are also five 'starter' sessions included here as examples of three-stage circle meetings. You know your children well and will be able to decide what is best for them at their current stage of development. Remember to remind the children about the ground rules and the five learning skills before you begin each session and use the lesson plans creatively by adapting them and mixing and matching as you please. You will soon become skilled at planning your meetings to suit the particular needs of your group/class of children and there are activities in the other sections of the book that can be incorporated into your circle meetings as appropriate.

All the Circle Time meetings are planned to meet the Early Learning Goals listed in the QCA document *Curriculum Guidance for the Foundation Stage* and each plan begins with a brief description of the relevant goal and its colour-coded stepping stone.

THREE-STAGE INTRODUCTIONS TO CIRCLE TIME

Box 5.1

TOMMY THUMB

ELG (early learning goal) for disposition and attitudes

Stepping stones	(Yellow) Have a positive approach to new experiences. (Blue) Show confidence in linking up with others for support and guidance.
Group size	Whole group.
Resources	None.
Introductory stage	Mime simple actions for children to follow, and identify areas of the body they are touching, e.g. tap your nose, touch your toes, clap your hands, stamp your feet, click your fingers, blink your eyes, shake your shoulders, wave your elbows.
	Follow with lots of praise about how well they did.
Middle stage	A musical hello, using the traditional rhyme:

> Tommy Thumb, Tommy Thumb,
> Where are you?

Substitute the first two words with:

> Hello ___ , Hello ___ ,
> Where are you?

The child replies, 'Here I am, Here I am.'

To which you respond, 'How do you do!'

Smile at each child and try to engage eye contact, perhaps using a handshake.

Continue around the circle until all the children have had a turn.

Repeat, asking the children to help you sing. Remind them that we say 'Hello' when we meet someone.

All the children can shake hands when 'How do you do' is sung.

Clap each child's name several times.

Ask the group to join in.

Use different tempos.

Closing stage/plenary	Congratulate the children for trying out a new idea and for joining in so well.

A musical goodbye, using the traditional rhyme:

> Twinkle twinkle little star.

Sing to each child:

> Now it's time to say goodbye (child's name), (child's name), wave goodbye.

Encourage the children to wave goodbye when their name is sung.

Congratulate the children for doing so well.

Box 5.2

BELONGING

ELG for self-confidence and self-esteem

Stepping stone	(Blue) Have a sense of belonging.
Group size	Four to ten children.
Resources	None.
Introductory stage	**Name clap** – The children say the name of each child in the circle in turn. As they say the name they clap the rhythm of the name. Congratulate them for knowing each other's names.

Middle stage   Sing the 'Belonging Song', to the tune of 'The Wheels on the Bus':

> Children in this class/group like to play, like to play.
> Children in this class/group like to play, all day long.

Add verses that mention the children by name and let the child choose their own activity, e.g.:

> Nazra in this class/group likes to skip.
> Leon in this class/group likes to paint.

Involve as many children as possible. Actions can be added.

Ask the children how many of them like to do the activities mentioned in the song. Call out the actions one at a time and get children to put their thumbs up if they do.

Box 5.3

FEELING HAPPY

ELG for behaviour and self-control

Stepping stone	(Yellow) Begin to accept the needs of others, with support.
Group size	Four to ten children.
Resources	A puppet. A talking object.
Introductory stage	**Catch a smile** – All the children and the practitioner stand up. The practitioner makes eye contact with a child and then smiles. The smiled-at child smiles back and sits down. Continue until everyone has had a turn.
Middle stage	Introduce the puppet and tell the children that he is feeling sad. Ask why he might be feeling sad. Then ask the puppet, who says that he is being left out of

games and no one listens to him. Ask the children what they could do to help him.

Round	'I could ___.'
	Can the children make their faces look sad? Now change to look very happy.
Closing stage/plenary	Explain to the children that we want all the children and adults in our group to feel happy, so we should try to help each other feel happy.
	Copy a ripple – The practitioner wiggles their fingers, explaining that they are making rain. The children copy. The practitioner changes the action to thunder, slapping their knees or waving their arms. The practitioner performs the various movements with their hands and ends by bringing out the sun by miming a circle with their hands. Everyone smiles.
	Sing 'If You're Happy and You Know It':

> If you're happy and you know it . . .
> Clap your hands, Stamp your feet, Shout 'I am'.
> If you're happy and you know it and you really want to show it.
> If you're happy and you know it . . .

Box 5.4

THINGS WE CAN DO

ELG for self-care and health and bodily awareness

Stepping stone	(Yellow) Demonstrate a sense of pride in their own achievement.
Group size	Four to ten children.
Resources	None.
Introductory stage	**Animal game** – The practitioner goes around the circle telling each child they are one of three animals,

e.g. duck, cow or dog. When their animal is mentioned the children make appropriate noises and when 'farmyard' is said all the animals make their noise.

Middle stage Tell the children you are going to sing a song about some of the things they can do.

Sing the chorus to 'Here We Go Round the Mulberry Bush'. After the chorus sing verses about things the group can do, e.g. wash our hands, eat our dinner, go to sleep, go for a walk. Include actions and ask the group for suggestions of things they can do.

Closing stage/plenary Congratulate the group for being able to do so many things. The practitioner and the children stand up and hold hands. They swing their arms and chant 'We are special.' On the word 'special', still holding hands, everyone raises their arms above their heads. They then lower their arms and repeat the sentence.

Box 5.5

SPEAKING AND LISTENING

ELG for sense of community

Stepping stone (Yellow) Make connections between different parts of their life experience.

Group size Four to ten children.

Resources A talking object.
A puppet.
Some music for musical statues.

Introductory stage Mime simple actions for the children to follow. Identify areas of the body they are touching, e.g. scratch your ear, touch your toes, rub your elbow, click your fingers, blink your eyes. Follow this with lots of praise about how well they did.

Middle stage	Introduce the puppet.
	Salt: Hello children my name is Salt. Before I came to the group today I had my breakfast, and I played with my car and I cleaned my teeth.
	Ask the children to think about one thing they did before they came to the group that they could tell Salt and the other children.
Round	'One thing I did was ___.'
	If the children want to elaborate, they can as long as the pace of the lesson is not lost.
	Thank the children for sharing.
Closing stage/plenary	Congratulate the children for joining in and speaking in the circle and for listening when other children were speaking.
	Tell the children they are going to play a game and they have to listen. They can dance/move to the music but, when it stops, they have to stay very still.

FULL CIRCLE TIME MEETINGS

Box 5.6

WHAT'S IN THE BAG?

ELG for disposition and attitudes

Stepping stone	(Yellow) Show curiosity. Demonstrate a strong exploratory impulse. Show a positive approach to new experiences.

57

Group size	Six to ten children.
Resources	A number of bags of different sizes, packed one inside the other with a favourite cuddly toy hidden inside the smallest one.
Preparation	None.
Meeting up	**Finger wiggle** – Smile at the child next to you and wiggle your fingers as if you are playing a piano. Let the child pass the wiggle on until it comes back to you.
Warming up	Using the talking object, ask the children to complete this round – 'My best toy is ___.'

Opening up	1	Tell the children that you are a bit worried because you cannot find your favourite cuddly toy.
	2	Tell them that you did find something rather strange when you were looking for it.
	3	You found a very big, very full bag that has something inside it.
	4	Pick up the big bag and show it to the children.
	5	Invite them to guess what they think could be inside.
	6	Allow them to come forward and have a look inside and take out one bag after the other until you have 'found' the cuddly toy.
	7	As you are doing this, use appropriate vocabulary – inside, hidden, smaller, bigger, etc.
	8	Share your joy at finding the cuddly toy and thank the child who found it for you.

Cheering up	Thank all of the children for helping you to look inside each bag until the cuddly toy was found.
	Pass a smile and a thank-you round the group.

Calming down

Wiggle your fingers very slowly and pass a slow finger wiggle round the group until it comes back to you, as you did in the meeting up stage. Then pass the cuddly toy round the group and let everyone give it a stroke.

Box 5.7

WHAT DO YOU NEED?

ELG for disposition and attitudes

Stepping stone	(Blue) Show an increasing independence in selecting and carrying out activities.
Group size	Six to eight children.
Resources	A selection of domestic items with which the children will be familiar – toothbrush, knife and fork, soap, bowl, slippers, etc. A tray to put them on.
Preparation	None.
Meeting up	**Copy me** – Guide the children through a mime of daily activities like cleaning their teeth. Talk them through as they copy your actions, such as cleaning your teeth or blowing your nose, etc.
Warming up	Using the talking object, ask the children to complete the sentence, 'I am good at ___.'
Opening up	Put the items and tray on the floor.
	1 Ask one child at a time to find you the item that is appropriate to a particular task.

2 For more able children you can vary the way in which you ask the question or ask children for more than one item.

Cheering up Point out to the children that they can do a great many things for themselves because they have just shown you a few of them.

Tell them to give themselves a clap for being so grown up and clever.

Calming down Put the tray away and ask the children to show you one more thing. Say that you want to see how they snuggle down at night and go to sleep. Let them curl up on the floor for a little while and then 'wake' them very quietly by gently whispering in their ears that it is time to wake up and go on to the next activity.

Box 5.8

WHO KNOWS WHERE?

ELG for disposition and attitudes

Stepping stone (Blue) Show confidence in linking up with others for support and guidance.

Group size Four to six children.

Resources Some familiar group/classroom toys.

Preparation Put the group/classroom toys in places where they are not usually kept but can be seen – window ledge, etc.

Meeting up Ask the children to point at items of their own clothing – 'Point to your socks, etc.' Then ask a particular child to find other children's clothing –

'Sara, find a pair of pink socks. John, find a pair of blue shorts.'

Warming up	Round – 'I have a ____ in my bedroom.'
	(Ask the children to tell the group one thing that they have in their bedroom.)

Opening up	1	Ask one child to choose a partner.
	2	Ask the pair to go and find one of the things that you have put in unusual places and bring it back to you.
	3	Do this until every child has had a turn at both choosing and seeking.

Cheering up	Congratulate the children on their skill at finding things.
	Thank them for working so well together.
	Point out that they are getting very good at doing more and more things for themselves and by themselves.
	Ask them to share other things that they can now do for themselves – find their own school bag or coat or put their own clothes in the laundry basket at home, etc.

Calming down	Tell the children that another thing that they can do all by themselves is calm down when they need to and that they do this by breathing slowly.
	Show them what you mean by sitting very still and quietly and letting your breath be steady and slow.
	Ask them to try this out.
	Sit quietly for a few minutes before softly telling them what the next activity will be.

61

Box 5.9

SHOW AND TELL

ELG for disposition and attitudes

Stepping stone	(Green) Display high levels of involvement in activities.
Group size	Four to six children.
Resources	A collection of ordinary useful objects from around the group/classroom or from home – paint brush, glue pot, washing-up liquid, wooden spoon, umbrella, toy hammer, etc. A tray.
Preparation	None.
Meeting up	Show everyone how to join in this rhyme. Let the words describe the actions. The mixing spoon goes round and round 　[make a stirring movement with one arm] It makes lovely slurping sound 　[make a slurping sound as you breathe in] Pour it on the baking tray 　[pretend to pour a bowl of cake mix into the baking tray] We're having chocolate cake today! 　[rub your tummy and look pleased]
Warming up	Using the talking object, ask the children to complete the sentence, 'My favourite colour is ___.'
Opening up	1　Put the items on the tray in the middle of the circle. 2　Ask one child to choose an item and give it to a pair of children who are sitting next to each other.

	3 The pair must then tell the group everything that they can about the item – what it is called, what they notice about it – hard, soft, cold, where it is kept, etc.
	4 Ask them to tell the group how the item is used and give prompts and help where necessary.
	5 Make sure that every pair of children gets at least one turn.
Cheering up	Congratulate the children on how much they know about the useful things that surround them in their daily lives and point out that they have learned a great deal about how things are used.
Calming down	Go through the warming up rhyme once again and then tell the children that they are going to rock a pretend baby until it is truly asleep in its cradle. Tell them that you will all hum together as you rock the baby and hum a song with which they will be familiar until everyone is calm and ready for the next activity.

Box 5.10

IT'S TIME TO SIT IN THE CIRCLE

ELG for self-confidence and self-esteem

Stepping stone	(Yellow) Separate from main carer with support.
Group size	Four to six children.
Resources	You will need to alert all members of staff that they will be called upon to join the group and introduce themselves.

63

Preparation   None.

Meeting up   Ask the children to join in this chant to the best of their ability. Put in names of staff and children as you go along.

> Let's all sit in the circle,
> Let's all sit in the circle,
> Let's all sit in the circle,
> With ___ and ___.
> Let's all sit in the circle,
> Let's all sit in the circle,
> Let's all sit in the circle,
> With ___ and ___.

Warming up   Using the talking object, ask the children to complete the sentence, 'At nursery, I like to play with ___.'

Opening up   1 Tell the children that there are many kind people at the nursery who would like to get to know them better.

2 Ask each member of staff to come and sit with the group and introduce themselves and talk a little about how long they have worked at the nursery, what kind of jobs they do and the ways in which they help children.

3 Encourage the children to ask questions if they are able to do so and, if not, ask them yourself, bearing in mind what you think the children would most like to know.

4 If children have older brothers, sisters or cousins who have previously attended your nursery, it is a good idea to make this connection for children.

Cheering up   Use this little rhyme to thank each member of staff for coming to your circle meeting. Substitute each person's name for 'Mrs Brown'.

Mrs Brown is here today
Mrs Brown is here today
We'll all clap our hands and say,
'Thank you, Mrs Brown.'

Calming
down

1   Ask the children to hold hands in the group.

2   Gently squeeze the hand of the child next to
    you and ask them to pass the squeeze on round
    the circle. (This may be difficult for some children
    so you could substitute a shake of the hand.)
    Repeat this with a smile and then with a
    'hello'.

3   Unclasp hands and thank the children for listening
    to each member of staff so well.

4   Remind them that all of the members of staff are
    there to make them feel happy at nursery school
    and that they can go to any member of staff
    whenever they need to during the day.

Box 5.11

INTO THE UNKNOWN

ELG for disposition and attitudes

Stepping stone	(Green) Take risks and explore within the environment.
Group size	Six to eight children.
Resources	A blanket or large cloth. A number of different objects from around the room – a trike, a picture, a story book, a purse, etc.

Preparation   When the children are elsewhere you will need to spread the objects across the floor and cover them with the blanket.

Meeting up   When the children are sitting in the circle, ask the children all to curl up in a little ball and wait until their name is called. Then say,

> *Teacher:* Where is Susie?
> *Susie:* Here I am.
> *Teacher:* How are you this morning?
> *Susie:* Very well, thank you.
> *Teacher:* It's very nice to see you today.

Repeat this song until every child has had a turn and change the command (wiggle your fingers) so that each child does something different.

Warming up   Using the talking object, ask the children to complete the sentence, 'I hang my coat on the ___ peg.' (This works if the pegs have different pictures/features to distinguish them.) At first, young children will tend to parrot the first statement made as part of a round, so the sentence needs to elicit a personal, individual response from each child.

Opening up   Choose each child in turn to wriggle under the blanket and bring out an object.

Ask them to show the group what they have found and ask them to talk a little about what the object does and how it is used.

Ask each child to show the group what they would do with it, if they are too shy to talk.

Ask them to put the object away in the right place and thank them for tidying up so well.

Tell the children that it must have been just a little bit scary to go under the dark blanket and wriggle around but that they did it very well.

Ask them to talk about other times when they have been scared of the dark and talk about ways of making it less scary.

Take suggestions from other children about coping strategies they have used to deal with fear.

Cheering up   Use this rhyme to the tune of 'Muffin Man':

> If you've been under the blanket today,
> Blanket today, blanket today,
> If you've been under the blanket today,
> Stand up and say 'Hoo-ray!'

Calming down   Tell the children that the blanket has another use because we can wrap ourselves up in it and feel nice and snuggly and warm.

Let the children curl up on the blanket until you go round and touch each child gently on the shoulder, which is the sign that they can get up very slowly and go to their next activity.

Box 5.12

WHOSE HOME IS IT?

ELGs for self-confidence and self-esteem

Stepping stone	(Blue) Have a sense of belonging. Show care and concern for self. Talk freely about home and community.
Group size	Six to eight children.
Resources	Pictures of people at home. Pictures from magazines would be quite sufficient. Pictures of animals in their homes (see p. 70). Some peaceful music.
Preparation	None.
Meeting up	To introduce the theme, teach the children this finger rhyme:

> Worms live in a hole.
>   [Wiggle your fingers downwards]
> A bird lives in a tree.
>   [Wiggle your fingers upwards]
> Fish live in the river.
>   [Wiggle your fingers horizontally]
> But home is the place for me!
>   [Point to self]

Warming up	Using the talking object, ask the children to complete the sentence, 'My front door is painted ___.'
Opening up	Draw the children's attention to the pictures of animals in their homes. Show them the ways in which the animals build homes that are suited to their needs.
	Tell them that we also need homes to keep us safe and warm and that we, too, share them with other people.

Tell them about yourself (or a made-up 'relative') and describe what goes on at breakfast time in your house – the rushing about, the fight for the bathroom, your baby brother refusing to eat his porridge, etc.

Then go round the circle and ask the children to contribute what they eat for breakfast or, if they are ready, funny stories such as a story about the day that the cat ate the bacon.

Give each child a turn, and encourage those who find it difficult to open up.

If you have children in the group who are possibly enduring difficult times at home, make sure that you help them to restrict themselves to 'hard' facts like 'We have cornflakes and chocolate milk for breakfast' so that they have contributed without needing to mention anything tricky.

Cheering up

Thank the children for being so very good at telling us interesting things and for listening so well.

Tell them that listening is very important at school and that they have managed it very well.

Let them give themselves a good clap.

Calming down

Tell them that you are going to do a different kind of listening now and that you want them to listen to a lovely peaceful piece of music.

Play the music until you see that the children are quietly relaxed and then take them calmly on to the next activity.

Box 5.13

DO YOU KNOW?

ELG for self-confidence and self-esteem

Stepping stone	(Blue) Have a sense of belonging.
Group size	Six to eight children.
Resources	A prepared set of questions.
Preparation	You will need to look around the room and prepare a set of questions at the right level for the children. (Some suggestions are included in the warming up section below.)
Meeting up	Prepare the children with this rhyme:

> I write with a pencil
>   [Mime writing]
> I draw with a pen
>   [Mime drawing]
> When I take the top off
>   [Mime taking the top off a pen]
> I put it on again.
>   [Mime putting it back on]
> I cut with the scissors
>   [Use two fingers to mime cutting]
> On paper so thin
>   [Hold out two hands, flat and close together]
> Then I pick up the pieces
>   [Bend over and pick up tiny pieces of paper]
> And put them in the bin.
>   [Cup hands together and then mime tipping paper into the bin]

Warming up	Using the talking object, ask the children to complete the sentence, 'Today, I am sitting next to ___.'

Opening up   1   Tell the children that you are going to ask them some questions and that they must listen carefully and put up their hand if they know the answer.

2   Ask questions about the nursery, such as: Where do we keep the glue pots? Who has a friend called Wayne? What is the name of the teacher who makes us our drink? Show me where we go when we want to be quiet? Who likes to play outside on the moving toys?

Cheering up   Congratulate the children for how well they know the nursery and each other. Point out that when they came everything seemed strange and that when we go to new places we are strangers, but that they are now part of everything and that makes it feel like a family in the group/classroom.

Send a little hug round the group because that is what families do.

Calming down   Ask the children to close their eyes and put their hands on their knees with palms facing upwards and their fingers slightly curled. This relaxes their shoulders and most children find it easier to sit still when in this position. Using a mood music cassette or a rain-stick encourage the children to close their eyes, listen and try to picture themselves playing in the sunshine somewhere nice.

After a couple of minutes, you can calmly bring them back to the room and thank them for an enjoyable circle meeting.

Box 5.14

WIND UP/WIND DOWN

ELG for self-confidence and self-esteem

Stepping stone	(Blue) Show care and concern for self.
Group size	Six to ten children.
Resources	A wind-up toy. A short piece of music that slows down at the end.
Preparation	None.
Meeting up	Use this action rhyme with the children: Ten little men 　[Hold up your fingers] And a great big key 　[Turn a heavy key with your hands] Will they go fast? 　[Wiggle your fingers very fast] Or will they go slow? 　[Wiggle your fingers slowly] Put them on the floor and then we'll know! 　[Walk your fingers across the floor in front 　of you]
Warming up	Using the talking object, ask the children to complete the sentence, 'I am wearing [insert colour] socks today.'
Opening up	1　Wind up the toy, but not too much!
	2　Show the toy to the children and let them watch as it slows down.
	3　Tell the children that, sometimes, we all get 'wound up' and need to 'wind down'. We call this 'calming down'. Has anyone ever been told to calm down? Would they like to tell us about it?
	4　Put the children in pairs.

5 Ask them to pretend that they have a big wind-up key on their backs.

6 One step at a time, ask them to plan a little dance that has four parts.

▶ First, they must wind each other up by turning the very heavy key on their partner's back.
▶ Then, they must move in a jerky, mechanical way, just like a robot.
▶ Now, they need to move more and more slowly until they have wound down. As they wind down, they must let their bodies become less stiff and more floppy.
▶ Finally, they need to move slowly, lower and lower, until they are lying on the floor, very still and calm.

Cheering up	Ask the children if they know any other ways to 'wind down' and if they would like to share them with the group by showing and telling. Thank everyone for sharing their helpful suggestions and discuss what you liked about them.
Calming down	Play the music and let the children dance until the music slows down and they relax on the floor for a few moments.

Box 5.15

SAME, SAME BUT DIFFERENT

ELG for self-confidence and self-esteem

Stepping stone	(Green) Have a sense of themselves as a member of different communities.
Group size	Six to eight children.

Resources	A copy of Red Riding Hood.
Preparation	None.
Meeting up	Look at the child who is next to you and give him/her a big smile.
	Ask them to pass the smile on to the next child and so on around the group.
	Repeat this but add the words, 'thank you for being friendly' to the round.
Warming up	Using the talking object, ask the children to complete the sentence, 'My favourite story is ___.'
Opening up	1 Read the story of Red Riding Hood.
	2 Ask the children if they have a grandma.
	3 Ask them if their grandmother lives in a cottage in the woods.
	4 If they say no, express surprise and ask them to tell you where their granny lives.
	5 Allow a number of children to tell you about their granny, how they travel to visit her, how often they see her, etc.
	6 Ask them if they know of any other 'old' people who live in their street.
	7 Can they tell you a little more about them?
Cheering up	Congratulate them for their interesting contributions and tell them that they are clearly very good at noticing things and excellent at sharing what they have seen.
	Let everyone clap themselves for being such clever children.
Calming down	Ask the children to close their eyes and put their hands on their knees with palms facing upwards and

their fingers slightly curled. This relaxes their shoulders and most children find it easier to sit still when in this position. Using a mood music cassette or a rain-stick encourage the children to close their eyes, listen and try to picture themselves playing in the sunshine somewhere nice.

After a couple of minutes, you can calmly bring them back to the room and thank them for an enjoyable circle meeting.

Box 5.16

HIDE AND SEEK

ELG for self-confidence and self-esteem

Stepping stone	(Green) Express needs and feelings in appropriate ways.
Group size	Six to ten children.
Resources	Pictures showing the six basic emotions.
Preparation	None.
Meeting up	Ask the children to listen carefully as you clap a rhythm and then to clap it back to you. Then clap a different rhythm and ask them to repeat that. Ask if anyone would like to have a go at clapping a rhythm for everyone to copy.
Warming up	Using the talking object, ask the children to complete the sentence, 'The best thing about the game [above] was ___.'
Opening up	1 One child is chosen to leave the group.

2   While they are not looking, give one of the cards to a child who must look at it carefully, check that they can 'read' the emotion it shows and then sit on the card to hide it.

3   The chosen child is then asked to rejoin the group.

4   The child who is sitting on the card must make an appropriate face and try to sit in an emotionally appropriate manner while everybody else copies them.

5   The chosen child then walks round the group and looks at everybody's face.

6   When they have guessed what mood is being conveyed they are to say, for example, 'You are looking very cross.'

7   You can then discuss the 'right' and 'wrong' ways to communicate each of these emotions.

Cheering up   Select a child who needs support or encouragement and tell the group about something that this child has done well this week. Say how pleased and happy this has made you and ask everyone to give them a big clap. Ask the children if anyone has done something to make them happy and would like to share it with the group. Praise their contributions.

Calming down   Send a smile round the group by smiling at the child next to you and asking them to pass it on.

Box 5.17

CAN I JOIN THE GAME?

ELG for self-confidence and self-esteem

Stepping stone	(Green) Initiate interactions with other people.
Group size	Six to ten children.
Resources	Two glove puppets. A small selection of toys.
Preparation	None.
Meeting up	Pass a smile round the group and then have a round where the children complete the sentence, 'I like to play with ___ because ___.'
Warming up	Using the talking object, ask the children to complete the sentence, 'My favourite food is ___.'
Opening up	1 Introduce the puppets to the children. For instance, Perry Pig and Jerry Giraffe.

2   Play out the following script with the puppets:

Teacher: Perry, you are looking very sad and lonely. What can have made you feel so sad?

Perry: I want to play with Jerry and the toys but he won't let me.

Teacher: Jerry, why won't you play with Perry today?

Jerry: Because I want to play with the toys all by myself.

Teacher: But, Jerry, I thought that Perry was your friend and friends don't make each other sad and lonely.

3 Ask the children what they think that Perry and Jerry should do. Take their suggestions, repeat and clarify them so that they are clear to all the children. Use the puppets to show the children how these suggestions work out in practice and add some more of your own by saying things like 'I was in the playground yesterday and I saw how Samantha joined in Kerry and Josie's game by offering to hold the rope. That was very clever of you, Samantha. Perhaps some of you might like to try something like that when you want to join in a game.'

Cheering up	Ask the children to join hands in a circle and sing this chant. At the end of each line, they raise their hands towards the ceiling and then lower them. At the end of the last line, they let go and point to everyone else in the group with a big smile.

I'm happy with my friends.
I'm happy when we play.
I'm happy with my friends.
And you're my friends today!

Calming down	**Breathing deeply** – Tell the children to take a deep breath while you count to five. Then, as you count back to one, ask them to breathe out slowly.

Box 5.18

IN THE LAND OF BLIMABOO

ELG for sense of community

Stepping stone	(Green) Have an awareness of, and show interest and enjoyment in, cultural and religious differences.

79

Group size	Six to twelve children.
Resources	A selection of dressing-up clothes.
	An example of music from another culture or time.
Preparation	None.
Meeting up	Pass a thumbs-up and a smile to the child next to you and then round the group.

Ask the children to join you in this traditional finger rhyme:

> Dance, thumbkin dance,
> > [Wiggle thumb]
> Dance, thumbkin dance,
> > [Wiggle the other thumb]
> Dance, you merry men, every one.
> > [Wiggle all your fingers]
> But thumbkin can dance alone,
> > [Wiggle thumb]
> Thumbkin, he can dance alone.
> > [Wiggle other thumb]

Warming up	Using the talking object, ask the children to complete the sentence, 'I can wiggle my ___ [nose, toes, fingers, etc.].'
Opening up	Use this script to lead the children into the activity:

> Once upon a time, long ago and far away from here there was a land called Blimaboo.
>
> The people in Blimaboo didn't dress the way that other people do.
>
> They may seem strange to me and you.
>
> But they like it that way in Blimaboo.

1	Choose a confident child to be a person from Blimaboo and ask them to stand in the centre of the circle.
2	Ask other children in turn to choose a hat, cloak, shoes and other items to 'dress' the person from Blimaboo.

3 Then ask the dressed child to go round the group, bow and say 'hello' to each child in Blimaboo language.

4 If you have time, you can repeat this with a person from another pretend land.

5 If you wish, you can give the children time to ask questions of each of their 'guests', such as 'What do you eat for tea?' 'Ants' eggs on toast.'

Most children need to have questions modelled by an adult before they can ask appropriate questions themselves. Be prepared for a lot of practice!

Cheering up	Congratulate the children on how nicely they welcomed the person from Blimaboo into their circle meeting. Tell them that we are all foreigners sometimes when we go to strange places and ask children to describe their experiences either on holiday or with people from other cultures. Praise them for their contributions.
Calming down	Play the foreign music and ask the children to sit quietly and listen carefully and to use their imagination to try and imagine the place where such music could have been made.

Box 5.19

KONRAD THE KING IS COMING TO VISIT

ELG for making relationships

Stepping stone	(Blue) Demonstrate flexibility and adapt their behaviour to different events, social situations and changes in routine.

Group size	Eight to twelve children.
Resources	Some dressing-up clothes. Pretend cups and saucers, etc. that you might need to entertain his majesty. A copy of Sleeping Beauty
Preparation	None.
Meeting up	Ask the children to stand up and pass a bow round the group.
Warming up	Sit down and do this round: 'If I met a king I would say ___.'
Opening up	1 Ask for a volunteer to be Konrad the King and dress them up to look very important and regal.
	2 Send the volunteer to stand outside the group for a while and ask the children for suggestions about how they should behave if a king came to visit them. Plan how you will behave and what you will say to the king and then invite him to visit you with due ceremony.
	3 Treat Konrad the King very royally until it is time for him to leave and go about his royal duties somewhere else.
	4 Ask the children if they can think of any other occasions when they must behave in a similar way – politely, quietly and carefully.
	5 Show them how you behave when you have to go and see someone important – make up a story about it if you wish but go into a little bit of detail.
Cheering up	Tell the children that you know that we all need to behave especially well sometimes but that you have seen and heard that they are very good at knowing when to be especially good and quiet.

Let them bow to each other and give themselves a big clap and a pat on the back.

Calming down	Remind the children of the story of Sleeping Beauty and especially about the part when everyone in the court fell asleep where they sat. Put on the quiet music and let them close their eyes where they sit until they are calm and peaceful.

Box 5.20

RUBBISH BUGS

ELG for behaviour and self-control

Stepping stone	(Blue) Show care and concern for others, for living things and for the environment.
Group size	Six to twelve children.
Resources	Two fluffy toys that will act as 'rubbish bugs'. A selection of pen tops, crisp packets and other 'litter'.
Preparation	Spread the rubbish around the room before the meeting.
Meeting up	Pass one rubbish bug round the group and ask each child to give it a stroke and say, 'Hello, how are you today?'
Warming up	Using the talking object, ask the children to complete the sentence, 'My favourite cuddly toy is ___.'
Opening up	1 Put the two rubbish bugs on the floor so that they are lying on their backs and looking very floppy.

2 Tell the children that these two fluffy animals are rubbish bugs and that they are very tired because they have had too much work to do.

3 Pick them up and ask them why they are so very tired and let them tell you that it is because they have been up all night making the room nice and clean and tidy and that, now, they need a rest and a good long sleep.

4 Ask the children if they know of anything they could do to stop the rubbish bugs from getting so tired.

5 Take suggestions and let children show each other where the rubbish you have scattered should be placed – felt pens in the pot, scrap paper in the recycling bag, crisp packets in the bin, etc.

6 With each suggestion, let the rubbish bugs sit up and hop about looking very pleased.

7 When you have received enough suggestions, ask the rubbish bugs how they are feeling now and let them show their appreciation for a good night's sleep.

Cheering up Tell the children that they have made the rubbish bugs so happy that they have made up a rhyme for the children. Would they like to hear it? Make up a tune for this song and sing it in a 'rubbish voice'!

> Rubbish bugs smile and grin
> When we put rubbish in the bin.
> Rubbish bugs wave and wag
> When we put the paper in the bag.
> We give them smiles
> We give them hugs
> We love to help the rubbish bugs.

Calming down   Ask the children to lie on the floor and wave their arms and legs in the air just like rubbish bugs. Then ask them to put their legs quietly on the floor followed by their arms and to lie quietly like a rubbish bug at the end of its long night's work. Let them lie quietly for a few minutes.

Box 5.21

STICK WITH IT

ELG for sense of community

Stepping stone	(Green) Have a positive image and show that they are comfortable with themselves.
Group size	Eight to twelve children.

Resources	Stickers with smiley faces drawn on them. A smiling puppet or picture of someone smiling. Cheerful music.
Preparation	None.
Meeting up	Divide the group into pairs. Tell them that they have to take it in turns to try and make their partner laugh. They can pull silly faces but not make physical contact. Their partner has to remain serious for as long as possible.
Warming up	Using the talking object, ask the children to complete the sentence, 'I can [run/jump/draw, etc.] very well.'
Opening up	1 Give each child a sticker still on its backing paper.
	2 Choose one child and ask them to unpeel the sticker and put it on someone else's jumper.
	3 As they do so, they need to say, 'I am giving you this because you are ___ [nice/my friend/good at helping me, etc.].' Give prompts if necessary.
	4 When each child has received a sticker, go round the group and ask them to repeat the reason why they were given the smiley face.
	5 Ask the children if they liked to receive the sticker and the kind words from their group/classmates and tell them that they can give other people this warm feeling at any time because all they have to do is smile and say something nice.
	6 Ask them if they can think of someone who might like to receive the gift of some kind words – such as their mum for cooking a good dinner – and tell them to try and remember to say something kind to everyone at home and at school every day and see how much happiness they can make all by themselves.

Cheering up   Tell the children that smiles are very 'catching' and a very good thing to share.

Tell them that you have a little rhyme about this and you want to teach it to them all.

Pick up the smiley puppet or show them the picture of a smiley person and say:

> Here's smiley Sue.
> What shall we do?
> Her smile is so bright,
> We are smiling too.

Calming down   Play the cheerful music and ask the children to move their arms and legs in a floating, light way to the rhythm of the music until everyone is in a happy frame of mind.

MEETINGS TO TEACH THE GOLDEN RULES

Box 5.22

THREE LITTLE KITTENS

Theme   We look after property, we don't waste or damage things.

Group size   Six to eight children.

Resources   None.

Preparation   None.

Meeting up   Tell the children that they are all going to be kittens and then go round the circle and tell each child what colour kitten they will be – white, black, brown. When you call out a colour, the children who are that colour must stand up. To develop this idea, next time you call

out a colour the children should change places
with someone who is the same colour by scampering
to their seat. This will mix up the group and ensure
that everyone is sitting next to somebody different.

Warming up Using the talking object, ask the children to complete
the sentence, 'If I was a kitten I would ___ [purr,
climb up the curtains, etc.].'

Opening up 1 Read the children this nursery rhyme:

Three little kittens they lost their mittens
And they began to cry,
'Oh mother dear, see here, see here,
That we have lost our mittens.'
'What, lost your mittens! You naughty kittens!
Then you shall have no pie.
Meeow, meeow, meeow,
No, you shall have no pie.'
The three little kittens, they found their mittens,
And they began to cry,
'Oh mother dear, see here, see here,
For we have found our mittens.'
'Put on your mittens, you silly kittens,
And you shall have some pie.
Purrr, purrr, purrr,
Yes, you shall have some pie.'

2 Ask the children to tell the rest of the group
about times when they, or members of their
family, have lost something important and
what happened because it was lost. Did dad
ever lose his car keys? Did mum ever lose her
glasses?

3 Prompt them by telling a story of your own if
necessary.

How did they go about sorting out the
problem?

How long did it take to find the lost items?

Were they ever found or did they need to be replaced?

Cheering up	Thank the children for their useful contributions and say that their families must be very pleased with them for helping to find things that were lost.
Calming down	1 Ask the children to sit very quietly and to shut their eyes.
	2 Tell them to slowly touch their elbows to make sure that they are still there.
	3 Ask them to gently touch their shoulders to make sure that they are still there and haven't been lost.
	4 Ask them to quietly touch their hair.
	5 Ask them to put their hands in their laps and gently wiggle their toes.
	6 Ask them to gently wiggle their fingers.
	7 Ask them to breathe very quietly for a moment or two and then to open their eyes and 'come back to the room'.

Box 5.23

ROCK-A-BYE BABY

Theme	We are gentle, we do not hurt anybody.
Group size	Six to eight children.
Resources	None.
Preparation	None.
Meeting up	Send a finger point around the group by smiling and touching something on your face – nose, mouth, ears, etc. The child next to you touches the same place and

then turns to face the next child, smiles and touches the same place. For a second round, turn, smile and touch somewhere else, the second child responding and so on around the group.

Warming up   Using the talking object, ask the children to complete the sentence, 'When I was a baby I couldn't do this ___ [walk, clean my teeth, etc.].'

Opening up   1 Ask the children what they know about babies and discuss what they have to say.

2 Talk about how babies like to be sung to sleep and that we have special songs called lullabies to help them calm down and feel sleepy.

3 Teach them this lullaby:

Rock-a-bye baby
Your cradle is green
Father's a nobleman
Your mother's a queen
And Betty's a lady
And wears a gold ring
And Johnny's a drummer
And drums for the king.

4 Ask them how this song should be sung. Should we sing loudly or quietly?

5 Agree that we need to sing quietly and that the baby needs to be held very gently as we sing.

6 Ask them to hold a pretend baby very gently as you sing the lullaby very softly and then to pretend that the baby has fallen happily asleep.

Cheering up   Thank the children for being so gentle with their baby.

Tell them that they have made the baby very happy and that it won't be squawking and screaming because it is happily asleep now.

Calming down   Tell the children to lie down on the floor and pretend to be babies themselves.

Sing the lullaby very softly and let them relax completely as you sing.

Box 5.24

I LOVE LITTLE KITTY

Theme   We are kind and helpful, we do not hurt other people's feelings.

Group size   Six to eight children.

Resources   Some peaceful mood music.

Preparation   None.

Meeting up   Go round the group and point to each child in turn and tell them that they are a mouse, a frog or a rabbit. When you call out 'rabbit', all the children who have that name must hop to another place. When you call out 'frog', all the children who have that name must jump to another place and, when you call out 'mouse', all of the mice must walk very quickly. You can do this more than once.

Warming up   Using the talking object, ask the children to complete the sentence, 'If I had a pet, I would like it to be a ___.'

Opening up   1   Tell the children that you are going to tell them a little poem about a kitten. It goes like this:

> I love little kitty,
> Her coat is so warm,
> And if I don't hurt her

She'll do me no harm.
So I'll not pull her tail,
Nor drive her away
But kitty and I
Very gently will play.
She shall sit by my side,
And I'll give her some food;
And kitty will love me
Because I am good.

2   Ask the children if they can remember any of the
kind things that the person in the poem does for
the little kitten.

3   Ask them to act out some kind things that we can
all do for a little kitten.

Cheering up   Ask the children to nominate other children in the
group who have been kind recently. Repeat the act
of kindness so that everyone is clear about what
has been done and give these kind children a big
clap.

Repeat this for members of staff.

**Calming
down**   Tell the children that we can be kind to ourselves
as well.

Show them one way in which we do this.

Tell them that it is called relaxation.

Put on the mood music and ask the children to lie on
the floor and let the music relax them. 'Let it relax
your toes. Let it relax your knees. Let it relax your
hands.', etc.

Box 5.25

WASHING DAY

Theme	We try to work hard, we do not waste time.
Group size	Six to ten children.
Resources	Some happy dance music.
Preparation	Make a note of children who have been working very hard recently. Try to find something positive to note down about every child in the group.
Meeting up	Hold up your hands and let your fingers wiggle as you bring them down. At the same time, make a 'shhhh' sound. Tell the children that this is the sound of rain on washing day.
	Let them join in as you do it again.
	Then turn to the child who is sitting next to you and do it for them. Ask them to pass this finger wiggle and rain sound round the group.
Warming up	Using the talking object, ask the children to complete the sentence, 'When it is wet and rainy, I like to ___.'
Opening up	1 Tell the children that you are going to tell them a little poem about an old lady who worked very hard so that she could look nice when she went out dancing. The poem goes like this:

> The old woman must stand
> At the tub, tub, tub,
> The dirty clothes
> To rub, rub, rub,
> But when they are clean,
> And fit to be seen,
> She'll dress like a lady,
> And dance on the green.

2 Show the children how people used to wash their clothes in a big tub and let them mime the hard work.

3 Then ask them to mime taking the heavy washing basket out into the garden and hanging all that wet washing on the line with big wooden pegs.

4 Then point out that all of that hard work was worth it because the old woman was able to dress like a lady and dance on the green.

Cheering up Tell the children that you have noticed that some of them have been working very hard lately.

Read out their names and the occasion when you noticed them trying really hard.

Ask them to give each other a big cheer.

Calming down Repeat the activity that was used for the 'Meeting up' phase of the session.

Box 5.26

THE EMPEROR'S NEW CLOTHES

Theme	We are honest, we do not cover up the truth.
Group size	Six to ten children.
Resources	A copy of The Emperor's New Clothes.
Preparation	Read this story to the children before your circle meeting.
	Make a note of times when the children have been honest and have it ready when you begin the meeting.

Meeting up	Ask all the children to stand up and pass a royal bow around the group. Say, 'good morning, [child's name]' or 'good afternoon' as you do so.
Warming up	Using the talking object, ask the children to complete the sentence, 'My favourite clothes are ___.'
Opening up	1 Recap the story of the emperor's new clothes and ask the children to act out different scenes from the story.
	2 Ask them if they have noticed just how many people lied to the emperor and make a list of all the characters including the crowd who cheered him as he walked through the streets.
	3 Ask them if they noticed who was the *only* person who told the truth.
	4 Tell them that the lies turned out to be very embarrassing for the emperor. How would they feel if someone got them into trouble by covering up the truth?
	5 See if anyone is brave enough to tell of situations when they got into trouble because someone else lied about them.
	6 Return to the end of the story and reread the part that tells of the dishonest tailors running away very fast.
Cheering up	Tell the children that we should all be honest and must try not to cover up the truth and praise them for times when they have done this difficult thing.
	Celebrate the incidents of honesty that you have noted down.
Calming down	Use the guided visualisation at the end of the book that is entitled 'The Palace' (see pp. 128–9).

Box 5.27

OLD KING COLE

Theme	We listen, we do not interrupt.
Group size	Six to twelve children.
Resources	A number of objects from around the room. (It doesn't really matter what they are.) A big comfortable cushion or a cosy chair. Some calming music.
Preparation	None.
Meeting up	Tell the children that you are leader of the orchestra and that they must copy what you do.
	Pretend to play different pretend instruments – piano, violin, trombone, etc. – and let the children join in with the actions.
Warming up	Using the talking object, ask the children to complete the sentence, 'The music I like best is ___.'
Opening up	1 Choose one child to be King Cole and let them sit on the big cushions.
	2 Tell the children that King Cole has been working very hard running his kingdom and now he needs a good rest.
	3 Tell them that you know just what King Cole likes to hear when he is tired because you have learned a poem about him.
	4 Read them the following nursery rhyme:

Old King Cole
Was a merry old soul,
And a merry old soul was he;

He called for his pipe,
And he called for his bowl,
And he called for his fiddlers three.
Every fiddler he had a fiddle,
And a very fine fiddle had he;
Oh, there's none so rare
As can compare
With King Cole and his fiddlers three.

5   Choose three children to play pretend fiddles for King Cole.

6   Ask the children if they think that King Cole is enjoying his well-earned rest.

7   Now give one of the group/classroom objects to a child who is still sitting in the circle and whisper that they must take this to King Cole. Ask them to hurry.

8   Do this again and again until every spare child has interrupted King Cole's peaceful rest.

9   Ask the children if they know how King Cole must be feeling now that his peaceful rest has been interrupted so many times.

10 Give them some vocabulary to describe how he must be feeling – irritated, annoyed, etc.

11 Tell them that we all feel like poor King Cole when people keep butting in and stop us from speaking or concentrating.

12 Ask them if they ever annoy their mums, dads or carers by interrupting.

13 Ask them if they have a brother or sister who interrupts when they are trying to say something and see if they can describe how it feels to be interrupted.

Cheering up   Thank the children for their wonderful acting and amazing fiddling skills.

If any children have done something excellent since the last meeting, this is the time to commend their good behaviour.

Calming down	Play the calming music and lead the orchestra again using appropriate instruments.

Chapter 6

Further creative approaches to Circle Time

USING THE DRESSING-UP BOX

Young children's social play may appear to be fraught with disagreements and hullabaloo but it is essential to their development because it teaches them to accept other people's points of view in a way that their interactions with adults could never achieve. 'Let's pretend' forms a large part of the social play of 3–5 year olds. This play is part fantasy and part imitative role-play and is often called 'socio-dramatic play' because it is both interactive and creative. When they act out their unscripted dramas, children are learning a number of vital social skills that include:

- ▶ How to improvise in conversations.
- ▶ How to make their conversations interesting and active.
- ▶ How to negotiate (often their play will begin with a 'planning stage' along the lines of, 'I'll be the witch and run around screeching and you'll be scared and then . . .').
- ▶ How to respond to the unexpected (because the agreed plan is abandoned!).
- ▶ How to 'get into the mind' of the character they are playing and act and think appropriately.
- ▶ How to use their imaginations to investigate a wide range of personalities and situations where possibilities are boundless.
- ▶ The opportunity to explore 'real' situations (like going to the dentist) that may cause fear or distress in a situation that is safe and comfortable.

How to use socio-dramatic play with young children

Children's aptitude for role-play and make-believe with objects and situations can easily be incorporated into your circle meetings and the dressing-up box will usually provide all the props you need to make your circle meetings truly magical! The following tips will help design your own role-play activities:

▶ **Use socio-dramatic play to stretch your children beyond their level of ability.** If you watch children when they engage in socio-dramatic play, you will quickly notice that they often assume roles that are beyond their current age and ability, which means that this play has the added benefit of raising self-esteem by allowing the child to feel stronger and more in control than they may feel in the 'real' world.

▶ **Use socio-dramatic play to give status to children who don't normally receive it.** All of your group will have a common understanding that you have all entered the land of 'let's pretend' and will happily accept that a less popular or shy child has become leader and king for a few minutes. Once the child is wearing the crown or costume, all the limitations of ordinary existence are removed and you will find hidden depths in even the most withdrawn children.

▶ **Make role-play a safe environment to explore contentious issues.** When taking a role, children often have the courage to say things that they would not dare to say in real life. You need to ensure that you plan well and keep control of events, but many children are prepared to 'pretend' to be afraid of the dark even if they are unwilling to admit to the same fear in real life, for instance, which means that you can discuss real issues inside the safe boundaries of imaginary play and thus alleviate fears and problems without embarrassing any of the children in your group.

▶ **Use simple props.** St George may have needed a large white horse, a full set of armour and a long sword to kill a dragon but a 4 year old can do it easily with a stick and a friend willing to roll over at the right time; therefore all you need to transform a shy child into Mighty Magician Whizzo, for example, is a bit of curtain or a rod with a star on the top.

That was the moment when Sam remembered that he'd left his new toy sports car at school . . .

▶ How do you think Sam felt when he remembered?
▶ What do you think Sam's mum and dad said to Sam?
▶ What can Sam do now to put it right?

USING STORIES TO TEACH SOCIAL, EMOTIONAL AND BEHAVIOURAL SKILLS

Throughout history, all over the world, stories have been used to teach children about Emotional Intelligence and the consequences of actions. Fables, folk tales, fairy tales and nursery rhymes still have this function but we now have wonderful new stories that support this tradition. Children love to hear stories and you often see them re-enact them in their free play. When stories are suited to the children's developmental level, they are able to relate to the action that takes place because they can see that their own real-life experience is very similar. If a story is very familiar or you read it just before your circle meeting, you can use its content to stimulate activities at any stage of Circle Time. When you select stories, it is useful to bear the following points in mind:

▶ Select books that are at the children's developmental level.
▶ Use books that are well illustrated with big pictures that can be shared by the whole group.
▶ Make sure that the characters have the qualities, good or bad, that you wish to explore.
▶ Many stories describe the consequences of actions. Make sure that you have chosen one that does so in a way that the children will understand.

Stories develop children's social, emotional and behavioural skills in a number of powerful ways:

▶ **Stories help children to organise and communicate their thoughts** – Narrative is a significant form of human

115

If you make the props too complicated they will get in the way of the lesson you are trying to teach, so keep them simple and allow each child's imagination to fill in the gaps.

▶ **Plan your role-play carefully.** What is the point you want to make? This is your focus and you need to be very clear about it. Fix it in your planning with a single sentence. It may be a practical issue such as, 'We share the playground toys', or, alternatively, it may involve a complicated moral issue like not kicking or pushing one another. If you need to examine such a complex issue, then you must choose a single, specific aspect of the issue and concentrate on that. The golden rule is, 'Keep it simple.' Don't try to focus on more than one part of the subject at a time or the children will become confused and learn very little.

▶ **Check that the children share your understanding of the keywords.** It is probable that one word will be pivotal in any assembly so it is vital that everyone has a common understanding of what you mean by it. It would, for instance, be futile to hold a circle meeting about co-operation if some of your children think that you are talking about the local Co-op shop! You need to explain, clarify and demonstrate the meaning of your keywords throughout the meeting if the value they represent is to be understood and practised by all children in the school.

▶ **Allow the children to develop your theme in their own way.** Play is essentially a creative activity and is important because it allows children to practise the vital skill of social improvisation. In other words, play is important precisely because it is unscripted. Your circle meetings may be planned and, to some extent, directed by you but you need to ensure that you give the children space to develop your theme in their own way. Obviously, this does not mean that you allow destructive behaviour to interfere with the role-play but, rather, that you offer a stimulus to get your children thinking but are prepared to celebrate the random factors that may be introduced by the more imaginative members of your group.

▶ **Join in.** Play is not something that we grow out of and is a fundamental human activity and a very healthy one at that, so put on a tiara yourself sometimes, wave your wand and show

the children that they are not the only ones who can create magic from the simplest of props. This will increase your understanding of the children you teach but, just as importantly, you will also find that you feel refreshed and vitalised by the experience.

The following activities can be used as part of your Circle Time meetings and can be adapted to meet the needs of your particular group.

Box 6.1

FROGS, PIGS OR DRAGONS

Resources	A wand.
What to do	1 Choose a child to be the wizard and hold the magic wand.
	2 Ask the wizard to go around the group touching each child with his magic wand.
	3 As he does so, he must give each child the name of an animal. (If the child playing the wizard is shy, you will need to help them here.)
	4 As each child is touched they must become the animal and move appropriately.
	5 You can choose to restrict your animals, if you wish, and have only farmyard, story book or cuddly animals. There are many possibilities.
	6 When the wizard says the magic word, 'stop' or taps the floor with his wand, all the animals have to go back to their seats.
	7 You can develop the role-play by adding details to the scenario. For instance, the wizard may want to take all of the animals to the beach or to a picnic

and then they need to behave in character while playing or eating.

8   You can ask the wizard to show how powerful he is by telling the group that if he touches them with his wand, they must instantly fall asleep or go back to their seat, or turn into another animal.

9   This activity is very empowering for shy or unassertive children.

Box 6.2

PRINCE/PRINCESS FOR THE DAY

Resources   A crown or tiara.

What to do   (This activity originated with a child who stated firmly that she was much better at counting when she was a princess and insisted on wearing her tiara whenever the counters were brought out! – Who could argue with such insight in one so young?)

1   Every child in the group is given a turn at being prince or princess for the day and wears a crown to indicate their status.

2   During the circle meeting, the child is invited to sit in the middle of the circle and the other children make positive comments about them – 'You are kind, you have nice hair, I like to play with you', etc. You need to be aware that some children are more popular than others and be ready with prompts to help the group out. It is a good idea to 'prime' the rest of the group with some good comments by modelling them yourself prior to the meeting.

3   When it is a child's day to be a member of royalty, they can receive certain privileges, like being first in the queue, sitting next to you at story time and choosing the book – you will have routines that can easily be adapted to the purpose. They can also receive a smiley card to take home.

4   Make sure that you keep a record of each child's day as the special child so that you know that you have been fair and given everyone the same number of turns.

Box 6.3

HOLD YOUR HAT

Resources	Coloured paper hats.
What to do	Activity one: **Model and mirror** – Put on a coloured hat and model the body language and facial expression appropriate to the colour. Ask the children to name the emotion that you are modelling. Ask for volunteers to wear the hat and mirror your behaviour.
	Activity two: **Reasons for feeling** – 'When I wear the red hat I am feeling angry and stomp about and frown. What could have happened to make me put on the red hat?' Children in this age group can usually offer **external** causes for emotions and benefit from having a go at suggesting **internal** causes. It will be up to you to coax and show them how it is done.
	Activity three: **Matching feelings** – 'I'm wearing the yellow hat because ___. Who would like to put on another yellow hat and finish the sentence, "I feel like wearing the yellow hat today because ___"?'

Box 6.4

HIDDEN TREASURE

Resources	A big box for a treasure chest.
	A number of small boxes.
	Some little things to put inside the small boxes – a holiday postcard, a small cuddly toy, a star, a 'magic' necklace that means that you can choose a game at playtime, a 'ticket' that lets you go and help the secretary in the office, etc.

What to do	1	Put each of the little 'gifts' into a small box.
	2	Put them all into the treasure chest.
	3	Put the treasure chest in the centre of the circle.
	4	Ask each child in turn to choose a box, open it and take out what is inside.
	5	Then they must choose another child who would like to have the gift. For instance, if they choose the picture postcard, they must give it to someone who would like a holiday. As they give the gift, they must say something nice to the child who receives it. They could say something like, 'Josie, I like you very much so I am giving you this picture of a nice beach.' No child can receive two gifts, so some children will need to be inventive.
	6	Then you can ask the children to pair up and play together with the two gifts.

Box 6.5

THE DRESSING-UP BOX

Resources   The dressing-up box.

What to do   1   Put the dressing-up box in the middle of the circle.

2   Say the following rhyme:

> Yellow socks,
> Green socks,
> Blue socks,
> Smelly socks
> Urrgh.
> > [Hold your nose]
>
> Wet socks,
> Dry socks,
> Old socks,
> New socks
> Mmmmm.
> > [Point to a child]

3   The child who has been pointed at may go to the dressing-up box and choose one thing. (It is a good idea to make sure that it is not too full because some children take a very long time to choose!)

4   Repeat until each child has chosen.

5   Then put the children in pairs and ask them to make up a very little play or game that uses their two items. In this way you can mix a fairy with a fireman or a king with a clown and the children will have to think laterally, discuss and negotiate before they can perform.

USING PUPPETS IN THE NURSERY

There are many advantages to using puppets in the group/classroom. Children love them and are immediately intrigued when they leave their cupboard and become suddenly alive. They have a habit of thinking aloud and like to give a running commentary about their inner lives. This teaches children a lot about intentions and emotions. Puppets also react in an exaggerated, immediate and visual way that makes their inner world easy to understand.

Another advantage of using puppets is the way that they are able to close the distance between you and the children with whom you are working. Once you have a puppet sitting on your lap, you can cross the generation gap and speak as a child. What is more, you can sit with your puppets and a script and nobody will complain because they will be so riveted by the puppet's antics that they won't notice that you are reading.

Puppets are particularly useful when you wish to model and talk about emotions that humans learn to hide, such as fear, uncertainty and embarrassment. They like to show these feelings and they love to ask children for advice about how to solve their problems. This helps to teach young children essential problem-solving skills and also gives them confidence in their own wisdom and ability to think things through. In doing so, the puppets also help children to understand the ways in which people are alike and different.

How to use puppets with young children

Puppets come in all shapes and sizes and you can even make your own. You may choose to work with a number of finger puppets or decide to invest in a couple of life-size characters. The following tips will help you to use puppets to their full advantage:

- ▶ Practise in front of a mirror so that you feel confident in manipulating the puppets and can give the story and group interaction your full attention.
- ▶ Involve the children in making the characters 'real' by letting them decide on names and personalities for them. They may need prompts, but this activity helps them to build characters that suit their needs. This also gives each character the

107

advantage of becoming like an extra pupil, friend and confidante for the children.

▶ Let your characters be one-dimensional and the embodiment of a few personality traits but not too many. Young children find it difficult to understand that people can hate and love all at the same time, which is why they like fairy stories where witches are all bad and princesses are constantly sweet and beautiful. When a character embodies a single, simple character trait they are able to comprehend its actions and reactions easily, which helps them to discuss the issue that you wish them to think about. So keep each puppet's character simple and reliably either good, bad, fearful or whatever you and the children choose them to be and always use them in that role.

▶ As time goes on, you can show the children how they can decide on the 'background' for each puppet and add new cousins or aunties to their repertoire of characters. This helps them to relate your circle meetings to their own lives and assists them to internalise the personal, social and behavioural lessons that you wish them to learn.

▶ Weave in problems and dilemmas that reflect the real, lived experience of your children. Let the children help you with this. This develops their cognitive skills and helps to teach them a great deal about how stories are constructed.

▶ Make your stories a kind of serial with a couple of episodes each week. This involves the children just as television series involve us and, if you sometimes end with a cliffhanger, you can be sure that your little audience will be very eager to sit down and hear the next instalment.

▶ Choose your key vocabulary in advance. Then you can show them how we use important words. Many children in this age group need to learn the words that go with nouns to make their meaning clearer, so decide what you want them to learn and make sure that you make the usage clear during the puppet show. You might decide to teach prepositions: about, above, across, after, along, around, before, behind, below, beneath, beside, between, beyond, by, down, in, inside, near, off, on, opposite, outside, over, past, since, through, under, underneath or up. Alternatively, you could structure your story around

the causative words that are so useful when we wish to discuss behaviour and its consequences: because, so, but, did, didn't. You might also wish to teach them opposites, such as fair/unfair, agree/disagree and right/wrong, that will help their moral development. Make a note of the words that you have chosen to use and make sure that you weave them into either the puppets' scripts or your role as narrator of their story. This will assist children's language development and will help them to explain themselves clearly, which, in turn, will make them feel more confident and calm both at home and in the school setting.

▶ Young children like the security of familiarity, so you will need to choose the kind of opening you will use. You might prefer 'Once upon a time' or another well-known way of starting a story, but it is important that you keep your beginning and ending rituals similar throughout the year so that the children have the sense of safety that predictability can bring.

▶ Keep your puppets in a special place that will be seen as their home. They need to retain their excitement so they shouldn't be constantly available. Keep them out of sight in a box or cupboard so that your children can feel the thrill of anticipation every time they emerge into the real world to tell of another escapade or situation.

The plot lines that follow are examples that you can adapt to your own needs. As your characters develop personalities and find their voice and background, they will demand that you make changes to any story and will insist that it is altered to meet their needs. As you practise this will become easier and it is well worth the effort. Each plot line will use puppets with different names but you, of course, will have your own names for the puppets in your setting.

Box 6.6

THE BIG, RED, FLUFFY CUSHION

Keywords   Fair/unfair
Share
Right/wrong

In Mrs Brown's quiet corner there was a blue carpet and ten soft cushions. Everyone went to the quiet corner for the register and to listen to stories and 'show and tell'. The ten cushions were all different and some had flowery patterns on them and one or two had tassels at every corner.

One of the cushions was quite a lot bigger than all the others and it was made from bright, red, fluffy material and that was the cushion that Wolf liked best, so he made sure that he was always first to the quiet corner so that he sat on that cushion and didn't have to sit on one with pink flowers on it. He was a clever wolf so he knew that when Mrs Brown picked up a story book she was going to call the children over and he made sure that he was ready to run in front of everyone else and get to the cushion first. If that didn't work, he would poke and prod whoever was on the cushion until they gave up and gave it to him, and, if that didn't work, he would sit on the edge of the cushion and, every time Mrs Brown wasn't looking, he would push and squeeze a little bit at a time until he was sitting right in the middle of that big, red, fluffy cushion looking very pleased with himself.

One day, Lamb was sitting on the big, red, fluffy cushion and Wolf prodded him so hard that it hurt and then he pinched him so that it hurt some more and then he kicked him with his sharp wolfy paws. Lamb hurt so much that he couldn't keep the tears in and he started to cry very quietly and hoped that no one would see. But Mrs Brown saw and she stopped reading the story and looked kindly at Lamb and said . . .

▶ What do you think Mrs Brown said?
▶ What did Lamb tell her?

▶ What did Mrs Brown do then?

▶ What do you think should happen to Wolf?

▶ What did he need to learn?

▶ What can we do to make sure that this story has a happy ending?

Box 6.7

THE TEDDY BEAR DUVET COVER

Keywords   Kind
Thoughtful
Want/need

One Tuesday, Charlotte's mummy came to pick her up from nursery and they went to Maisie's house for tea. All the way there, they giggled and messed about in the back of the car until Charlotte's mummy told them to be quiet and then they made faces at each other and tried to giggle quietly so that Charlotte's mummy wouldn't hear.

When they got to Maisie's house, they played tea parties with her dolls and watched the television for a while before Maisie said, 'Let's go upstairs and play with my cuddly toys.' Maisie had a big bedroom and a bed that was made to look like a princess's bed and on the top Charlotte saw a beautiful duvet cover that was pink and white and had pictures of princesses and mermaids printed all over it.

As soon as she saw it, Charlotte wanted to have a duvet cover just the same because she thought it must be the very best duvet cover in the whole wide world.

When she got home she told her mummy all about the lovely duvet cover and her mum said that she would ask granny and grandpa to buy her one for her birthday.

A few weeks later, it was Charlotte's birthday. Granny and grandpa came round for tea and they had a cake with candles that granny had

made especially for Charlotte. Then grandpa gave her a present and sat back and smiled as he watched her open it. Charlotte prodded and pressed and she felt that the present was soft and she felt very excited. But when she opened it she saw that it wasn't a lovely pink and white duvet cover with princesses and mermaids on it. It was a yellow duvet cover with teddy bears holding red spotted balls and big smiley faces.

Charlotte looked at granny and grandpa and saw them smiling at her and she burst into tears and ran upstairs to her bedroom.

▶ What happened to make Charlotte cry?
▶ What do you think Charlotte's mummy will ask Charlotte to do?
▶ Can you show me what she will say to granny and grandpa?

Box 6.8

JOY AND THE PRINCESSES

Keywords   Kind/unkind
                Problem
                Think and find a way

One day Joy was all by herself at nursery when she saw Mary and Kerry playing in the dressing-up corner. She went over to them and asked if she could join in.

'No,' said Kerry. 'We are playing at being princesses and there can only be two of us so go away.'

So Joy went and sat by herself and watched them playing. They had long pink dresses on and crowns on their heads and they were making tea with the tea set and drinking it together.

She sat and felt lonely for a while and then she had an idea. She walked up to the dressing-up corner and quietly put on a fairy

outfit that had a sticky-out skirt and silver wings. She found a fairy wand and then she danced round and round the two princesses and waved it over the teacups.

'What are you doing?' asked Mary. 'We said you couldn't play.'

'I'm the special fairy,' said Joy 'and I've come to magic your tea into spell juice that tastes much better than tea.'

▶ How did Joy feel when Kerry and Mary wouldn't let her play?

▶ Can you show me how she must have looked?

▶ What do you think we should say to Kerry and Mary?

Box 6.9

THE MUDDY SHOES

Keywords   Forget/remember
                Obey/disobey

It was the day of Aunty Sheila's wedding and everybody was getting ready at Tom's house. Tom's mum was having her hair done and his sister, Jane, was getting dressed up in the bridesmaid's dress that they'd been making for months in the living room. There were flowers everywhere and plates of sandwiches all over the kitchen.

Tom was feeling very uncomfortable because they had made him wear a new suit with long trousers and a white shirt with a little tartan bow tie.

Everyone was busy and no one was taking any notice of Tom so he had a sandwich from one of the plates and wandered outside into the garden in his smart wedding outfit.

Today was a lovely hot day and all his family said it was a perfect day for a wedding, but yesterday had been wet and there on the path Tom saw a great big muddy puddle.

Tom looked at the puddle for a minute or two and then he looked inside to see if anyone was watching. No one was, so Tom walked back up the path a little way and then he turned and ran . . . and jumped!

▶ What do you think happened next?
▶ What do you think Tom's mum said?
▶ How do you think Tom felt?

Box 6.10

THE SPORTS BAG

Keywords	Forget/remember
	Listen
	Disobey
	In trouble

One day, Sam's dad gave him a blue toy sports car that he got from the filling station when he went to buy his petrol. Sam was very proud of that car and he asked his mum if he could take it to nursery to show all his friends. His mum said, 'No, Sam. They have lots of toy cars at nursery and yours will get mixed up with theirs and it will take us ages to find it.'

But Sam didn't listen to his mum and the very next day he hid the car in his pocket and took it school after he'd been told not to. All that afternoon, he played with Jon with the cars and the road map that goes on the floor and they had a lovely time until Mrs Brown called them over to the quiet corner for a story. Sam was in such a hurry that he forgot all about the new car and he ran over to the cushions and listened to the story and then his mum came to take him home for tea.

When his dad came home from work, he said that he'd decided to get Sam another car when he went to get some more petrol and he asked to have a good look at the blue toy sports car to make sure that he bought a different one next time because two different ones are much better than two the same.

communication through which we can organise and communicate our beliefs, thoughts and experiences. If you look back over the conversations you have had in the last 24 hours, you will quickly notice that you were telling stories in almost every conversation! We construct stories about our experiences because it is a very effective way for us to communicate with one another and helps us to sequence our thoughts and make sense of our lives. Children need to learn this aspect of social interaction.

▶ **Stories increase children's vocabulary** – Children who can tell you how they feel are less likely to act out their feelings. Authors can't act out, they have to tell us what is going on using language, and children learn this vital vocabulary as they sit listening to the stories you tell.

▶ **Stories teach problem-solving skills** – Stories are often about transformation, which can only be achieved if the main character overcomes problems and obstacles. This teaches children that we all need to be motivated and overcome setbacks if we are to achieve our goals. Once the obstacles are overcome and the story has come to its conclusion, you can encourage your children to evaluate strategies that were used and to consider the consequences for the characters.

▶ **Stories inspire and teach by example** – Stories are often about brave people who achieve through perseverance or intelligence. These characters are role models and motivate children to emulate their heroes, set goals and strive to reach them.

▶ **Stories are therapeutic** – When they listen to a story, children know that it isn't quite real but they may also know that they have experienced something very similar. This offers them a place of safety because they can listen to the problem that the character faces and talk about these difficulties without having to describe their own problem. The changes that the character goes through can be explored in a manageable way and the resolution at the end offers a troubled child hope that they will also find a way to overcome their difficulties.

You will need to bear the following points in mind if you wish to use stories to teach social, emotional and behavioural skills:

▶ **Keep the group size small** – Your children will get the most from the story if they can see the illustrations clearly and discuss the book in a relaxed way, so a group of five or six is ideal.

▶ **Prepare the children for the story** – Children need to identify with the characters if they are to listen well and gain from your storytelling session. Before you begin the story, it is a good idea to have a brief discussion about their own experience of events that are similar to the ones that you know will crop up in the story. For instance, if the story is about a new baby, you can ask if anyone has a new baby at home and ask if it was hard for them to get used to.

▶ **Reflect on the issues raised at the end of the story** – This activity can be usefully done during your Circle Time meeting, so ensure that the story is fresh in the minds of your children. You can recap on the story and encourage children to share their comments, opinions and queries. You can guide this discussion and focus their minds on either emotional issues or the consequences of actions or the moral message embedded in the text.

▶ **Encourage active engagement** – Young children love to act out a story and this helps them to internalise what they have heard. You can use your Circle Time meetings to encourage this active engagement by:

- Allowing them to re-enact it using the dressing-up box.
- Using puppets and toys.
- Using the dialogue but adding gestures and body language – How do you think the king must have looked when he roared and shouted, 'Who has hidden my golden crown?'
- Work out plays that investigate what would happen if . . .? For instance, what would happen if the ugly sisters went to live with Cinderella at the palace?

The following activities can be used in your Circle Time meetings and can be adapted to suit the needs of your particular group. They use classic fairy tales because these stories are usually plentiful in nurseries, but your bookcase will be full of well-written modern stories that can be used in the same way.

Box 6.11

CINDERELLA

Group size	Six to eight children.
Resources	Some toy mice A toy lizard.
Preparation	Read the story of Cinderella to the children before this activity. (Details vary from version to version and you may need to adapt the activity to suit the version you are using.)

What to do	1	Ask the children if they know any words that tell us what kind of person Cinderella is. Give prompts if necessary and talk about the way in which she cares about the people and animals around her. Ask two or three children to show you how she cares for the mice and lizard – they can either use toys or work in pairs to do this.
	2	Ask the other children how it makes them feel when they watch Cinderella being so kind to the animals. Would they like to be looked after by Cinderella if they were little furry creatures?
	3	Talk about the way in which the ugly sisters and the wicked stepmother treat Cinderella and ask some children to act out this behaviour. How does this make the spectators feel inside? Do they feel unhappy and tight or worried? Would they like to live in the same house as the ugly sisters? Why not? How long do they think they could stand it before they wanted to cry and run away?
	4	Cinderella put up with it for a very long time and she never stopped being good and as cheerful as she could manage. Do the children think she is a weak person to put up with ill-treatment or is she strong?

5   Ask two children to act out the ugly sisters going to the ball with their noses in the air and ask the rest of the group to pretend to be Cinderella in her rags, watching them leave.

6   Can they show how she must be feeling? Do they know any words that describe that kind of feeling? Prompt them if necessary. Repeat any good suggestions and thank the child who has supplied them.

7   Ask the children to act out Cinderella's surprise when the fairy godmother suddenly appears.

8   Can any of the children suggest why she has chosen to be kind to Cinderella?

9   Do they think that the fairy godmother would be kind and caring towards the ugly sisters? Why not? Repeat any good suggestions and praise the child who has supplied them.

10   Point out that it is just the same in real life. When someone is kind and caring, they make us feel warm and happy and that makes us more caring in return.

11   Finish the session by playing some happy music so that the children can dance as if they are at the ball. Teach them to bow to each other as the dance begins because this is a very royal thing to do.

Box 6.12

HANSEL AND GRETEL

Group size   Six to ten children.

Resources   Beanbags and cushions.

119

Preparation		Read the story of Hansel and Gretel before this activity. (Details vary from version to version and you may need to adapt the activity to suit the version you are using.)
What to do	1	Recap the first part of the story.
	2	Scatter the cushions to make a 'path' through the forest.
	3	Select two children to be Hansel and Gretel and give Hansel the beanbags for pebbles.
	4	Tell Hansel to drop the beanbags one by one along the path and then lie down with Gretel and wait for the moon to come up.
	5	Announce that the moon has risen and that they must find their way home by following the trail of beanbags.
	6	Thank Hansel for being such a clever brother and looking after his sister so well.
	7	Recap the part of the story where the children are imprisoned in the gingerbread house.
	8	Select two children to re-enact how Gretel saves her brother from being a witch's dinner.
	9	Thank Gretel for being such a clever sister and looking after her brother so well.
	10	Point out to the children that Hansel and Gretel both take their turn at helping one another.
	11	Ask them to share ways that someone has helped them recently and show your appreciation for all contributions.
	12	Ask them for suggestions of the things that they are able to do to take their turn at being the helper rather than the helped.
	13	Celebrate and praise them all for their helpfulness and remind them that this is how we show that we care about one another.

Box 6.13

PUSS IN BOOTS

Group size	Six to ten children.
Resources	None.
Preparation	Read the story of Puss in Boots before this activity. (Details vary from version to version and you may need to adapt the activity to suit the version you are using.)
What to do	1 Ask the children to show you different ways in which cats behave – sleep, purr, wash, play, sleep some more!
	2 Recap the story of Puss in Boots and say that this is a very special cat. Can the children tell you about any of the wonderful things that this cat can do?
	3 Choose one or two scenes where the cat does something to help the miller's son and ask the children to re-enact them showing just how clever this cat can be.
	4 Ask one child to be the fierce ogre and another to be Puss in Boots. Who is big and who is small? Who would we all expect to win the battle that they have with one another?
	5 So how is it that the cat wins and not the ogre? Help the children to come up with the answer that the cat wins by keeping his cool and using his brain.
	6 Tell them that this is the best way of dealing with trouble.
	7 Think of some difficult situations and ask them how the ogre would deal with them. Then ask them

for suggestions for how a clever, thoughtful, cool cat would deal with them.

8   Give the children some examples of situations that are proving problematic in your nursery and role-play 'cool cat' ways of dealing with them effectively. These could include:

▶   Children snatching toys.
▶   Children refusing to share.
▶   Children disrupting others' play.
▶   Children feeling lonely or afraid.

Box 6.14

THE FROG PRINCE

Group size	Six to ten children.
Resources	Three big envelopes containing pictures of: (1) a kitten; (2) a puppy; and (3) a gerbil.
Preparation	Read the story of the Frog Prince before this activity. (Details vary from version to version and you may need to adapt the activity to suit the version you are using.)
What to do	1 Recap the story and ask the children to act out the part where the princess discovers that keeping her promise has brought her a magnificent reward!
	2 Ask the children if it is possible to keep a frog as a pet and if they have any suggestions to show how this might be done.
	3 Explain that you are going to pass round the first envelope. Let the envelope be passed until the following rhyme has finished:

What will you lose?
What will you keep?
It's your turn to choose,
Take a peek, [child's name].

4   Then pick a child to come forward and choose one of the large envelopes and share the picture with the group.

5   Ask the children if they would like to keep whatever animal is shown in the picture. Where would you keep it? How would you keep it safe?

6   Repeat this with the other two big envelopes.

7   Then say to the children that sometimes we need to keep things that we can't exactly see. Just as the princess did, we have to try to keep our promises. When do we make promises and why do we need to keep them? Introduce the phrases, 'to give your word' and 'to keep your word'.

8   How do we feel when someone breaks their promise? Stress that a promise must be freely given but, once it is spoken, we need to try our best to keep it.

9   Reflect with them on how the princess tried to break her promise and how she would not have been able to save the handsome prince if she had not been persuaded to keep it.

10   Ask the children if they have ever been asked to keep a promise. Was it hard to keep? Ask if anyone would like to share their experiences. Celebrate and praise any contributions that you receive.

WHAT ARE GUIDED VISUALISATIONS?

A guided visualisation is like a journey to the health-giving parts of our imagination. Just our imagined fears and anxieties can make us tense and sick, so our imagination has the power to calm and heal us and it is this aspect of our mind that is activated when we are led through a visualisation. This kind of visualisation is deeply relaxing because our attention is focused and we are required to sit very still and concentrate on the images that the guide puts into our minds. The guide speaks very slowly in a soothing voice and shows us how to create calming and affirmative images that we can recall and reuse in times of stress. Children are asked to close their eyes and put their hands in their laps and it is important that they concentrate on the task of emptying their minds of all emotions and thoughts except for the image you are building for them.

Each visualisation is designed to help children to experience a quiet 'now' moment after all the activity and excitement of the circle meeting. Mood music can be used to enhance the calming effect of the experience and there are many to be found in your high-street music shops. The following pointers will help you to guide your visualisations more effectively:

- ▶ Speak in a calm rather flat voice throughout.
- ▶ Speak slowly and clearly.
- ▶ Pause frequently so that children have the opportunity to 'make' the picture you are describing.
- ▶ Harness their imagination by using the stories that you have recently read to them.
- ▶ Make sure that all the images you create are peaceful, positive and happy.
- ▶ Ensure that the children are sitting comfortably and are not too close to one another.
- ▶ Keep distractions to an absolute minimum.
- ▶ Prepare your script in advance so that you do not lose your way and convey uncertainty or awkwardness.
- ▶ Leave spaces for the children to fill. You want them to be calm and still but you also need them to be actively involved in each visualisation, so it is important that you leave some aspects of the story open for them to make their own choices.

For instance, if the visualisation requires them to imagine a cuddly toy, it is better not to describe it in too much detail. Then the children have the opportunity to choose the toy that they would most like to cuddle up to.

The following scripts can be used as part of your Circle Time sessions and adapted to suit the needs of your particular group.

Box 6.15

THE TREE

1	Sit with both feet on the floor. Make sure you are comfortable and warm and will not be disturbed.
2	Close your eyes and sit very still.
3	Listen to your breathing. Can you feel the air going in and out? Just listen to your breath for a moment and let your mind become very still.
4	Take a long slow breath and let it out very gently, like this. Your breathing is slow and calm. Your mind is calm. Calm and slow. Calm and relaxed.
5	Pause.
6	Think about your feet. Make sure that they are very flat on the floor. Pretend that you are a tree and the roots of the tree are growing down into the ground. They are strong and they are going deep, deep into the earth that feeds them with water from the raindrops.
7	Pause.
8	You are a beautiful tree and you can feel a gentle breeze blowing all around your branches. You are a strong tree and all of your leaves are green and bright.
9	Pause.

10 A little bird comes to sit in your branches and it sings a lovely little song. The bird is very happy to be in your tree. It sings because it is happy. The bird has feathers of many bright colours.

11 Pause.

12 Now it is time for you to turn back into a boy or girl again. Gently let the bird fly away to another tree. Watch it fly away in the sunlight.

13 Shake your shoulders and arms.

14 Jiggle your fingers and toes.

15 Wiggle your knees and your elbows.

16 Open your eyes when you are ready and sit quietly for a moment.

Box 6.16

THE PRIZE

1   Sit with both feet on the floor. Make sure you are comfortable and warm and will not be disturbed.

2   Close your eyes and sit very still.

3   Listen to your breathing. Can you feel the air going in and out? Just listen to your breath for a moment and let your mind become very still.

4   Take a long slow breath and let it out very gently, like this. Your breathing is slow and calm. Your mind is calm. Calm and slow. Calm and relaxed.

5   You are in a room full of people but it is very quiet. You are sitting in a row of chairs and your loved ones are all there with you. Everyone is looking towards a big stage where an award is going to be given out.

6   Pause.

7   The man on the stage stands up and reads out the name of the winner of the prize.

8   The name he calls out is yours. You are the winner.

9   All of your family look round and give you a big smile.

10   Pause.

11   You walk to the front and up on to the stage and everyone is clapping and saying, 'well done'. You feel very proud of yourself because you know that you have worked hard and you have made your family happy.

12   Look at your prize. It can be any prize that you want it to be. Sit for a few moments and see the prize in your imagination.

13   Pause.

14 Now it is time for you to walk back to your seat. Take your time and hold up your prize for everyone to see. Begin to notice sounds around you.

15 Shake your shoulders and arms.

16 Wiggle your fingers and toes.

17 Wiggle your knees and your elbows.

18 Open your eyes when you are ready and sit quietly for a moment.

Box 6.17

THE PALACE

1 Sit with both feet on the floor. Make sure you are comfortable and warm and will not be disturbed.

2 Close your eyes and sit very still. Listen to your breathing. Can you feel the air going in and out? Just listen to your breath for a moment and let your mind become very still.

3 Take a long slow breath and let it out very gently, like this. Your breathing is slow and calm. Your mind is calm. Calm and slow. Calm and relaxed.

4 You are walking in a beautiful garden. Can you see all the flowers? What colours are they? Can you smell them?

5 It is the garden of a palace. It is a wonderful palace like the ones you see in fairy stories. Can you see the towers and flags and windows? You spend a little time looking at the palace. What do you see? You are quite safe here.

6 Pause.

7 The king and queen come out of the palace doors and walk towards you. You look at their golden crowns and their fine clothes. What colours are they wearing? Can you hear the

'swish, swish' of the queen's dress as she walks along the pathway? They are smiling and you know that they are pleased to see you.

| 8 | Pause. |

| 9 | As they get nearer, they bow and say, 'Hello, how nice of you to come and visit us.' Then the king hands you a present. It is something magic and amazing. What does he give you? You hold it in your hands and look at it. You feel very happy. |

| 10 | Pause. |

| 11 | Now it is time to bring your present home. You bow to the king and queen and wave goodbye. |

| 12 | Pause. |

| 13 | Take your time to come back to the room. Begin to notice the sounds around you. |

| 14 | Wiggle your fingers and toes. |

| 15 | When you are ready, you can open your eyes. |

Box 6.18

GREEN GRASS

| 1 | Sit with both feet on the floor. Make sure you are comfortable and warm and will not be disturbed. |

| 2 | Close your eyes and sit very still. Listen to your breathing. Can you feel the air going in and out? Just listen to your breath for a moment and let your mind become very still. |

| 3 | Take a long slow breath and let it out very gently, like this. Your breathing is slow and calm. Your mind is calm. Calm and slow. Calm and relaxed. |

4   You are walking on green grass. You are at the park and the sun is shining. What can you hear? Can you hear the children playing?

5   Pause.

6   Look up into the sky? Can you see little white clouds or is the sky very blue? You feel very calm and happy.

7   Pause.

8   You hear someone calling your name. It is someone you know very well. It is someone who loves you. They are calling you over for a picnic. You feel very happy and you run over to join them. They smile at you and you smile back. You sit down and eat your picnic.

9   Pause.

10   Now it is time for you to come back to the room. Take your time and begin to notice the sounds around you.

11   Wiggle your fingers and toes.

12   When you are ready, you can open your eyes.

Index

Jenny Mosley's whole school Quality Circle Time model

What our training can do for you

Headteachers and OFSTED have reported that the Quality Circle Time model helps schools to find success in their policies for:

Emotional Literacy	Positive Behaviour	Racial Harmony	Creativity
PSHCE	Anti-Bullying	RE	Staff Health and Well-being
Citizenship	Drugs Evaluation	Speaking and Listening	Work/Life Balance

Jenny Mosley's model for raising the self-esteem of adults and children has been established for nearly 20 years. The highly successful programme has been implemented in thousands of schools nationally and around the world.

To date, Jenny Mosley Consultancies have worked with 142 of the 154 LEAs in England, 28 of the 29 authorities in Scotland and 13 of the 22 authorities in Wales. Our work has been recognised by the DfES in five guidance documents issued to schools and LEAs.

Currently we are working with the Primary National Strategy to make clear how the model fits into the exciting and visionary initiative. It is also recognised by the National Healthy Schools Standard.

The impact of the Quality Circle Time model is recognised by many – from government agencies to key individuals including David Blunkett, David Puttnam and Cherie Blair. Visit http://www.circle-time.co.uk to read more.

We have a dynamic and inspirational team of consultants who are highly experienced at both working with schools and delivering workshops and keynote speeches at national and international conferences.

Our most popular training courses include . . .

Quality Circle Time masterclass

This day is suitable for those who have the skills of Circle Time and introduced some strategies but now want to build on these. The aims of this day will:

- Broaden and increase the scope of Quality Circle Time by adding new branches of ideas to the already established 'trunk' of the model.
- Provide more exciting games and creative ideas to promote social, emotional and behavioural skills (SEBS).
- Support the further development of children's imagination and emotional literacy.

Train the trainers

We have successfully delivered this 5-day in-depth course for nearly 15 years. Without proper training, ideas and methodologies can become diluted and distorted. This course can equip individuals to teach key features of this powerful model in the philosophy and psychology of Jenny Mosley's approach.

Additionally, this course can be hosted by an LEA for their own personnel. It ensures that everyone starts at the same point, allowing them to support each other. They also become a member of the Quality Circle Time network – a forum for sharing good practice that has many other benefits.

Achieving excellence through valuing individuals

From time to time we all need to evaluate our current practice and look at ways forward. This day will help you:

- Unite all your staff in a clear vision of respect and valuing of themselves and others.
- Evaluate the impact of your current behaviour and PSHCE policy.
- Work together as a positive and energetic team.

Create happier lunchtimes and playtimes

If a child is unhappy at lunchtimes and playtimes they are unhappy at school. This day aims to:

- Re-energise and improve playtimes, wet playtimes and dining halls to promote safe, co-operative and creative play.
- Inspire the whole staff to want to promote a positive lunchtime policy and to integrate it into your PSHCE and Circle Time policy.
- Build the self-esteem of the supervisors.

For further information please contact the Training Department, Jenny Mosley Consultancies by phone 01225 767157; fax 01225 755631; email circletime@jennymosley.co.uk

Jenny Mosley Consultancies, 28a Gloucester Road, Trowbridge, Wiltshire BA14 0AA

About *Nursery World*

Nursery World is the only weekly magazine for the childcare and early years education sector, and will keep you up to date with all the latest news, views and changes in government policy. Each week there are also advertisements for hundreds of job vacancies.

You'll find a wealth of practical content including:

- in-depth coverage of the Foundation Stage curriculum and Birth to Threes
- full projects plus ideas for outdoor activities, display and music.

The magazine also contains special eight-page 'All About . . .' guides on subjects such as learning through play, plus free posters.

There is also plenty of advice on working with parents, with guides and posters that can be photocopied or displayed for parents to read.

Other regular series provide information about good practice, child behaviour, inclusion, careers and training.

Nursery World also publishes a range of special supplements including Nursery Business, Nursery Equipment, Nursery Topics, Nursery Chains and Training Today.

You can buy *Nursery World* from your newsagent every Thursday – or take out a subscription by calling 0870 444 8628 or ordering online at www.nurseryworld.co.uk.